ASHE Higher Education Report: Volume 35, Number 3
Kelly Ward, Lisa E. Wolf-Wendel, Series Editors

Ethnic and Racial Administrative Diversity: Understanding Work Life Realities and Experiences in Higher Education

Jerlando F. L. Jackson

Elizabeth M. O'Callaghan

#43299954 92

Ethnic and Racial Administrative Diversity: Understanding Work Life Realities
and Experiences in Higher Education
Jerlando F. L. Jackson and Elizabeth M. O'Callaghan
ASHE Higher Education Report: Volume 35, Number 3
Kelly Ward, Lisa E. Wolf-Wendel, Series Editors

ISSN 1551-6970   electronic ISSN 1554-6306   ISBN 978-0-4705-8814-7

The ASHE Higher Education Report is part of the Jossey-Bass Higher and Adult
Education Series and is published six times a year by Wiley Subscription Services,
Inc., A Wiley Company, at Jossey-Bass, 989 Market Street, San Francisco,
California 94103-1741.

For subscription information, see the Back Issue/Subscription Order Form
in the back of this volume.

CALL FOR PROPOSALS: Prospective authors are strongly encouraged to contact
Kelly Ward (kaward@wsu.edu) or Lisa Wolf-Wendel (lwolf@ku.edu). See "About
the ASHE Higher Education Report Series" in the back of this volume.

Visit the Jossey-Bass Web site at **www.josseybass.com.**

Printed in the United States of America on acid-free recycled paper.

The ASHE Higher Education Report is indexed in CIJE: Current Index to Jour-
nals in Education (ERIC), Current Abstracts (EBSCO), Education Index/Abstracts
(H.W. Wilson), ERIC Database (Education Resources Information Center),
Higher Education Abstracts (Claremont Graduate University), IBR & IBZ: Inter-
national Bibliographies of Periodical Literature (K.G. Saur), and Resources in
Education (ERIC).

Advisory Board

The ASHE Higher Education Report Series is sponsored by the Association for the Study of Higher Education (ASHE), which provides an editorial advisory board of ASHE members.

Contents

Executive Summary

Although most colleges and universities have paid increased attention to providing access for people of color, key stakeholders—from taxpayers to students—remain concerned about institutional commitment to diversity. This concern is largely based on the lack of structural diversity evident on most college and university campuses. Although institutions have generally focused on access for people of color with respect to students and faculty, less attention has been placed on increasing diversity in administrative and decision-making ranks. The true test for a commitment to a diverse workforce at an institution is its demonstrated support of the recruitment, hiring, training, professional development, promotion, and career success of administrators and academic personnel of color. Accordingly, engagement, retention, and advancement for administrators of color should be included in the overall efforts of the college or university and considered another metric for an institution's commitment to diversity.

Research on the experiences of administrators of color, while emerging, is limited but essential to gaining a fuller and more balanced understanding of the increasingly diverse academic workforce. Accordingly, conditions under which administrators of color are most likely to remain, develop, and advance professionally in administrative careers in higher and postsecondary education institutions are discussed. Key policies and practices are identified to help colleges and universities increase the overall representation of people of color and improve their working conditions. A model developed by the lead author (the engagement, retention, and advancement of administrators of color model) was used to guide the synthesis of the monograph.

This monograph, organized into five chapters, is intended for policymakers, administrators, faculty, researchers, and governing boards interested in improving work conditions for administrators of color while also developing methods to increase administrative diversity at their respective institutions. It will also be useful for graduate students focusing on careers in higher and postsecondary education. The focus is primarily on relevant literature on administrators of color in higher and postsecondary education, with an emphasis on developing a clear synthesis of this research to inform effective practices to achieve ethnic and racial administrative diversity. Literature from other fields of study is also included to provide an external perspective on the challenges associated with people of color in administrative positions. The monograph addresses several major questions:

How diverse are the administrative ranks at colleges and universities?

What barriers may be preventing people of color from entering college and university administration?

What coping strategies are the most useful for aspiring administrators of color?

What institutional approaches may yield the most promise in helping colleges and universities increase ethnic and racial administrative diversity?

The first chapter introduces the monograph and outlines the next four chapters. "Status of Ethnic and Racial Diversity in College and University Administration" presents a descriptive analysis of the higher education workforce by race and ethnicity using national data. "Barriers Encountered by Administrators of Color in Higher and Postsecondary Education" identifies the myriad barriers previously identified in the literature. The next chapter synthesizes key factors associated with the engagement, retention, and advancement for administrators of color, and the final chapter provides conclusions and implications for future research, policy, and practice.

Foreword

Diversity is an increasingly vital objective in higher education. Although past rationales for this effort included the need to affirmatively remedy legacies of discrimination and to prevent historically disadvantaged groups from remaining disadvantaged, colleges and universities now more commonly connect diversity to the very heart of their institutional missions. Indeed, accreditation agencies require postsecondary institutions to be more attuned to how diversity is manifest in their mission, curriculum, and the representation of students and faculty. Most postsecondary institutions acknowledge the educational value of diversity in promoting a multiplicity of perspectives in classrooms and across campus, and they recognize the social value of diversity in preparing students to live in a pluralistic and multicultural democracy. One important piece of the diversity puzzle comes from having leaders who are from diverse racial and ethnic backgrounds. Although most of the attention on research and policy is focused on students and faculty, the diversity of administrators is equally important—but often ignored. In this monograph, Jerlando Jackson and Elizabeth O'Callaghan gather together the latest research and data available to help colleges and universities recruit and retain a more racially and ethnically diverse group of administrators. They make the case that having institutional leaders who represent historically underrepresented groups is an important diversity metric that deserves our attention.

This monograph is written to assist administrators, faculty, and graduate students to understand how diverse colleges and universities are at the administrative ranks, the barriers that prevent racially and ethnically diverse individuals from becoming administrators, the factors that affect the retention of administrators of color, and an overview of institutional initiatives that can aid in the successful recruitment and retention of administrators of color. Jackson and O'Callaghan focus on administrators at all levels—from presidents to athletics administrators to student affairs professionals. They root their argument in the notion of representative bureaucracy, that is, the importance of having leaders who represent the demographic composition of their constituency groups. Administrators at colleges and universities play a key role in shaping policy and practice and in building stronger institutions: who is hired to fill these key leadership roles is important. Having people of color stay in these roles is equally important.

This monograph serves as a helpful companion piece to other monographs published in the last few years, including *Diversity Leadership in Higher Education* by Adalberto Aguirre and Rubén Martinez (Volume 32, Number 3), *Are the Walls Really Down? Behavioral and Organizational Barriers to Faculty and Staff Diversity* by Alvin Evans and Edna Chun (Volume 33, Number 1), and *Bridging the Diversity Divide: Globalization and Reciprocal Empowerment in Higher Education* by Edna Chun and Alvin Evans (Volume 35, Number 1). Taken together, these monographs provide insight into the underrepresentation of people of color in leadership positions, the barriers they face, and, most important, how to address these concerns proactively. The focus on theory, research, and practice in all these monographs is a strength. This monograph by Jackson and O'Callaghan is particularly helpful in providing concrete ideas that institutions can employ to recruit and retain administrators of color. Among the suggestions include leadership training, mentoring programs, support groups, and targeted professional development opportunities.

Presidents, provosts, policymakers, researchers, governing boards, human resource and diversity practitioners, administrators, affirmative action officers, and faculty and staff committed to furthering their institutional progress on diversity will find this monograph a valuable resource. Because the monograph presents new data, reviews of existing research, theory, and practical suggestions, it will be useful to diversity task forces and councils, multicultural centers, search committees, and Equal Opportunity staff. Moreover, it is a good monograph for graduate students and higher education scholars to use as an example of how to synthesize current literature and theory as a means to inform practice and improve institutional effectiveness.

Lisa E. Wolf-Wendel
Series Editor

Acknowledgments

The authors are indebted to support systems that provided space to develop and write this monograph. Jerlando F. L. Jackson wishes to thank both the Wisconsin Center for the Advancement of Postsecondary Education at the University of Wisconsin–Madison and the National Center for Institutional Diversity at the University of Michigan for funding and resources to complete this project. He would also like to thank his family and friends for support throughout the duration of this project. Elizabeth M. O'Callaghan would like to thank the Department of Educational Leadership and Policy Analysis and the Media, Education Resources, and Information Technology Library at the University of Wisconsin–Madison for providing the necessary space and resources to begin this project. Professors Carin Clauss and Linda Greene from the University of Wisconsin Law School were especially helpful by sharing their insights regarding the complicated intersections among race, ethnicity, and the workplace.

Dedications

Jerlando F. L. Jackson would like to dedicate this monograph to Will Jackson, his Grandfather—the Patriarch of the Jackson Family. He passed away during the completion of this project. May his leadership be forever remembered.

Elizabeth M. O'Callaghan would like to dedicate this monograph to her father, Patrick J. Mooney, a retired social worker who spent his career working to provide equal access to educational opportunities for all students. His work is an inspiration to her.

Published online in Wiley InterScience
(www.interscience.wiley.com) • DOI: 10.1002/aehe.3503

Introduction, Context, and Overview

A LTHOUGH MOST COLLEGES AND UNIVERSITIES have given increased attention to providing access for people of color, key stakeholders—from taxpayers to students—remain concerned about institutional commitment to diversity (Cabrera and others, 1999; Holmes, Ebbers, Robinson, and Mugenda, 2000; Jackson and Rosas, 1999; Minor, 2008). This concern is largely based on the lack of structural diversity evident on most college and university campuses (Hurtado, Milem, Clayton-Pedersen, and Allen, 1999). Although institutions have generally focused on access for people of color with respect to students and faculty, less attention has been placed on increasing diversity in the administrative and decision-making ranks (Jackson, 2002). Researchers who monitor higher and postsecondary education have tagged access, retention, and advancement for administrators of color in predominantly White institutions as an area of concern and a hot topic for debate (Bennefield, 1999). Research-based responses to questions on these issues have redirected attention toward considering the presence of administrators of color, particularly in senior-level positions, as a key indicator of institutional commitment to diversity (Davis, 1994; Jackson, 2001).

The higher and postsecondary education literature contains a growing body of empirical and practical knowledge on administrators of color (Jackson and Flowers, 2003). One major challenge for colleges and universities to achieve administrative diversity is using past research studies to build a conceptual framework for understanding these challenges while at the same time producing useful knowledge for policy implementation. This problem is significant because in 2003 people of color represented 16.9 percent of the full-time administrators in higher education, compared with 82.7 percent for Whites (numbers do not add to 100 because 0.4 percent of full-time administrators were from foreign countries [Cook and Codova, 2006]). The literature has also suggested that attention to workplace experiences is warranted. Empirical accounts of the work realities for administrators of color in higher education have found less than desirable work arrangements.

A series of articles in premier higher education news venues (such as *The Chronicle of Higher Education* and *Diverse: Issues in Higher Education* illustrate well the work-related challenges encountered by administrators of color in higher education. June (2007) reports on the state of affairs regarding diversity among college presidents, noting that the profile of the typical president has remained the same over the past twenty years. That is, the typical president is a married, older White male with a doctorate. Minority representation in the college presidency has lagged behind White women as well. Prior experience as a president is increasingly becoming a preference, thus calling into question the future for people of color in these positions who are less likely to have that previous experience. Similar dynamics are expressed in athletics (Suggs, 2005); few people of color are rising to top jobs in athletic administration because they are not in areas that lead to these positions (such as marketing, business affairs, and rules compliance). In most cases, people of color are tracked into positions that focus on academic advising and life-skills counseling. Moore (2005) documents the internal struggles that some people of color experience relative to feeling qualified or prepared to apply for senior-level administrative positions, which sometimes cause people of color to remove themselves from the job search process.

Key empirical studies (see Davis, 1994; Konrad and Pfeffer, 1991; Moore and Wagstaff, 1974) have called for action to improve work conditions (silent discrimination) and representation (access to executive-level positions) for administrators of color, particularly at predominantly White institutions. In particular, Myers and Sandeen (1973) presented issues that still exist today. That is, people of color represented only 13.7 percent of the student affairs workforce, and 46 percent of the institutions surveyed did not have *any* African American professionals. Wilson (1977), in a follow-up study using the same survey and sampling technique, identified a decrease in representation for people of color in student affairs to 13.1 percent in 1974 (12.4 percent in 1998; see the following chapter 2 for a full analysis). These historical statistics have decreased over time, thus signally that significant disparities still exist for administrators of color regarding their overall representation and experiences.

This monograph is intended for policymakers, administrators, faculty, researchers, and governing boards interested in improving work conditions for administrators of color while also developing methods to increase administrative diversity at their respective institutions. It will also be useful for graduate students focusing on careers in higher and postsecondary education. The focus is primarily on relevant literature on administrators of color in higher and postsecondary education, with an emphasis on developing a clear synthesis of this research to inform effective practices to achieve ethnic and racial diversity among administrators. Literature from other fields of study is included; however, to provide an external perspective on the challenges associated with people of color in administrative positions, several major questions are addressed in this monograph:

How diverse are the administrative ranks at colleges and universities?

What barriers may prevent people of color from entering college and university administration?

What coping strategies are the most useful for aspiring administrators of color?

What institutional approaches may yield the most promise in helping colleges and universities increase ethnic and racial administrative diversity?

The Importance of Workforce Diversity in Higher and Postsecondary Education

At least two concepts, among others, such as social justice not discussed in this monograph, support the rationale for a racially and ethnically diverse workforce in higher and postsecondary education: representative bureaucracy and retention. These two concepts are representative (although not all encompassing) of our core argument for understanding racial and ethnic workforce diversity. Representative bureaucracy serves as an easy-to-understand heuristic tool that describes the importance of the representativeness of leaders. Our focus on retention is to highlight the omission of administrators of color in the dialog on the academic success of students of color and to speculate how the insertion of this group in the retention planning might take form.

The theory of representative bureaucracy is a core topic of public administration (Meier and Stewart, 1992); recently, it has also been applied to higher education research (see Flowers, 2003; Jackson, 2004b). The theory of representative bureaucracy posits the importance of having leaders, administrators, or policymakers that represent the demographic composition of their constituency groups (McCabe and Stream, 2000; Meier, 1975, 1993a, 1993b; Meier and Stewart, 1992). In defining the fundamental principle of representative bureaucracy, Meier and Nigro (1976) asserted that if the ethnic composition of administrators is similar to that of the general public, then the decisions made by these administrators would be responsive to the desires of the public. Two types of representative bureaucracy are apparent: passive representation and active representation (Meier and Bohte, 2001). Passive representation refers to similarities in demographic characteristics between administrators and constituency groups. Active representation refers to situations in which administrators work to further the needs of a particular group that may or may not share their same demographic characteristics.

Retention for people of color in higher and postsecondary education has received increased attention in the last decade (Cabrera and others, 1999). As noted earlier, the majority of this literature focused on students and faculty of color. Thus, access and retention for these two groups have been used to inform conversations of representation and diversity (Crase, 1994; Flowers, 2004–2005). These have made a glaring omission—the representation for administrators of color (Davis, 1994; Jackson, 2001). Previous research by the first author of this monograph presents a depiction of both a physical (numerical representation) and metaphorical (authority and control representation) relationship among the three targeted groups (students, faculty, and administrators) if all three are included in the representation and retention process (see Figure 1).

Students of color represent the bottom of the pyramid for two reasons: they ideally should be the largest people-of-color group represented on campus, and they are the foundation of any measure of racial and ethnic diversity. Faculty

FIGURE 1
Three-Tiered Approach to Institutional Diversity

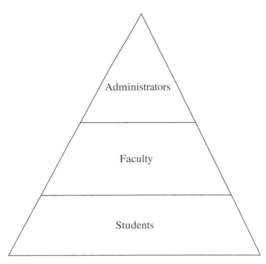

Administrators

Faculty

Students

Source: Jackson, 2006b.

are in the middle of the pyramid because research suggests that faculty of color can enhance the enrollment and retention of students (Turner and Myers, 2000) and may help attract administrators of color as well. Administrators of color are at the top of the pyramid because they generally represent the smallest group related to representation at predominantly White institutions and because they are involved in policy development and implementation that can shape the representation of the other two groups. According to Jackson (2001), engagement, retention, and advancement for administrators of color should be included in the overall efforts of the college or university and considered as another metric for an institution's commitment to diversity.

Literature and the Integrated Review

The authors reviewed the literature on administrators of color in higher and postsecondary education for inclusion in this report, using a list of terms related to the domains of interest to identify relevant articles. The following terms were selected and included in the search strategy: Blacks, African American, Asians,

Hispanics, American Indians, administrator(s), higher education, and postsecondary education. Computerized advanced literature searches of the Education Resources Information Center database using these terms were conducted. This extensive search of the literature yielded 136 studies that used administrators of color as a unit of analysis (Black/African American female athletic administrators and Latinos in executive positions in higher education). Although these articles served as the core body of knowledge, research literature (thirty-eight studies were identified for inclusion) that focused on administrators of color in other settings was used to supplement understanding (business, school leadership, and health administration). In addition, research that does not address administrators of color directly but provides important and appropriate insight into administrative work was included to ensure a balanced perspective. Thus, forty-eight articles focusing on traditional and general leadership topics were included in this review.

Reviews of research are a fundamental activity in the social sciences; they often precede major research studies and are also done as independent scholarly work (Cooper, 1982; Jackson, 1980). Using the tradition of integrative research reviews, this monograph summarizes and critiques the literature on administrators of color in higher and postsecondary education. Most important, these works are synthesized and interpreted to inform future research by scholars and improve performance of practitioners. Significant effort has been made to examine and critique theoretical assumptions and frameworks as well as methodical approaches as they relate to the examination of administrators of color in higher and postsecondary education. The identification of micro- and macrothemes embedded in the literature will help institutions work toward more inclusion. In line with the work on integrative reviews, this book provides "enriching perspectives on meanings and circumstances" that seek to "break down boundaries, and cause things (or thinking) to expand" (Eisenhart, 1998, p. 394). The goal of using this approach is to extrapolate theoretical and empirical perspectives on administrative diversity to better understand the current body of knowledge.

Chapter Overviews

This monograph is organized into four additional chapters. The following chapter, "Status of Ethnic and Racial Diversity in College and University Administration," presents a descriptive analysis using national data of the administrative workforce in higher education by race and ethnicity. "Barriers Encountered by Administrators of Color in Higher and Postsecondary Education" identifies the myriad barriers previously identified in the literature. "Factors Influencing Engagement, Retention, and Advancement for Administrators of Color" synthesizes key factors associated with those topics. The final chapter provides conclusions and implications for future research, policy, and practice.

Status of Ethnic and Racial Diversity in College and University Administration

The employment of administrators of color has remained fairly consistent over the past three decades with regard to representation (Jackson, 2002; Konrad and Pfeffer, 1991). Studies have found that, historically, White males were represented more in upper-level positions, while people of color were represented more in lower-level positions. In the past three decades, the number of administrators of color, including those in upper-level administration positions, has increased (Powell, 1991; Wilson, 1989). Caution is needed when looking at these advances for people of color in key administrative positions; however, because the data may obfuscate two types of occupational segregation, one by institutional type, the other by position held. For example, although the representation of people of color is rising, historically a larger proportion of administrators at historically Black colleges and universities have been White, compared with the people of color at predominantly White institutions (Konrad and Pfeffer, 1991). Second, although the American Council on Education produces an annual status report, data on administrators do not provide position-level detail except for college presidents. Moreover, data are not disaggregated by area of control (academic, student, or administrative affairs). This monograph provides an analysis of people of color who are academic and student affairs leaders in various institutional types.

Barriers Encountered by Administrators of Color in Higher and Postsecondary Education

Research-based and anecdotal evidence suggests that predominantly White institutions are ineffective, or marginally successful, at providing access to and retaining administrators of color (see Abney and Richey, 1991; Bridges, 1996; Brown and Globetti, 1991; Jackson and Flowers, 2003). Research (Davis, 1994) has suggested that administrators of color eventually become disenchanted with predominantly White institutions and often move to institutions that were historically created for individuals of their own racial or ethnic group (for example, Hispanic-serving institutions and historically Black colleges and universities) or leave higher education altogether. The reasons administrators of color take these actions can be considered barriers to career advancement and success.

Several barriers to career advancement previously identified in the literature include lack of job access, the glass ceiling, lack of opportunity for advancement, lack of professional identity, lack of a visible career path, poor working conditions, inadequate compensation, competition from outside the academy, and competition from within the academy (Barr, 1990). This monograph discusses three types of barriers that prevent administrators of color from achieving consistently high levels of professional success: social barriers, organizational or institutional barriers, and internal barriers. It also includes a brief discussion of legal and conceptual frameworks often cited in research on the underrepresentation of people of color in higher education: affirmative action, disparate impact theory, underutilization analysis, the theory of a representative bureaucracy, and the glass ceiling.

Factors Influencing Engagement, Retention, and Advancement for Administrators of Color

American colleges and universities have been transformed in the past generation from a racially and gendered homogenous population to a fairly diverse one, although not yet in proportion to the general population (Cohen, 1998; Thelin, 2004). College access for people of color expanded greatly from the 1960s through the 1990s (Harvey, 2002; Nettles and Perna, 1997). This phenomenon has resulted in more students of color attending predominantly White institutions than ever before (Allen, 1992). Research on the experiences of these students has surged; for example, the relationship between student experiences and contact hours with professionals on campus (faculty and administrators) (Pascarella and Terenzini, 2005) and the experiences of students of color in relation to faculty have recently been more fully incorporated into the literature base (see Flowers, 2002; Flowers and Pascarella, 2003). Research on the experiences of administrators of color, however, is limited but essential to gaining a more full and balanced understanding of the increasingly diverse academic workforce (McCurtis, Jackson, and O'Callaghan, 2009). Accordingly, conditions under which administrators of color are most likely to remain, develop, and advance professionally in administrative careers in higher and postsecondary education institutions are discussed in this monograph. Key policies and practices are identified to help colleges and universities increase the overall representation of people of color and improve their working conditions. A model (engagement, retention, and advancement of administrators of color) developed by the lead author (Jackson, 2004a; Jackson and Contreras, forthcoming) was used to guide the synthesis of the monograph.

Concluding Remarks Regarding the Importance of a Diverse Administrative Workforce

To understand the role diversity plays in strengthening the intellectual growth and environment at colleges and universities, institutions seek to diversify all levels of participation. As such, key stakeholders see the potential benefit of including diverse approaches to leadership and policy development to build stronger institutions. The final chapter provides implications for future research and recommendations for effective practices that will lead to ethnic and racial diversity among administrators. Where possible, recommendations for specific administrative tracks (academic, student, and administrative affairs) are provided as well. In short, institutions should not just be satisfied with "making a minority hire." The true test for a commitment to a diverse workforce at an institution is its demonstrated support of the recruitment, hiring, training, professional development, promotion, and career success of administrators and academic personnel of color.

Status of Ethnic and Racial Diversity in College and University Administration

L ONGSTANDING CONVENTIONAL KNOWLEDGE holds that people of color are underrepresented in administrative positions in higher education (Konrad and Pfeffer, 1991). It is difficult to provide a statistical breakdown for the participation of people of color in administrative positions, however, because these data are not readily available. The intent of this chapter is to address this gap in knowledge to provide a grounded context for understanding the challenges and opportunities for people of color in administrative positions. Specifically, descriptive national-level data highlight the status of people of color in comparison with Whites on various demographic and related characteristics (employment status and gender). Analyses of the higher education administrative workforce include both academic leaders and student affairs practitioners. In the context of this chapter, academic leaders constitute the positions that traditionally oversee the academic mission of the institution (college presidents, provosts, and department chairs), usually selected from or concurrently holding faculty rank. Student affairs practitioners traditionally oversee academic support services for learning out of the classroom (dean of students, director of housing, and director of admissions). These two administrative groups were selected because their functions are unique and specific to college and university administration.

Data for this chapter are from two national datasets: the National Study of Postsecondary Faculty (NSOPF:99) and the National Association of Student Personnel Administrators (NASPA) Salary Survey for 1999.[1] We used 1999 data because it was the only year for which we could secure data for both groups. The data presentation is organized separately for each database to

---

present a clear discussion. Likewise, the discussion is arranged across three domains: individual and demographic variables (age, gender, and highest degree); job-relevant variables (principal activity, program area, income, rank, and publications and presentations); and institutional variables (Carnegie classification, institutional control, institutional type, and region).

In an effort to provide a national context for the landscape for full-time administrators in higher education, McCurtis, Jackson, and O'Callaghan (2009) conducted a twenty-year descriptive and trend analysis of this group. They identified a 51 percent increase in full-time administrative positions between 1983 (117,486) and 2003 (177,724). To illustrate the underrepresentation of administrators of color, they found that in 2003, 17,228 or 10.31 percent were African American or Black,[2] 7,006 or 0.04 percent were Hispanic, 4,813 or 0.03 percent were Asian Americans, 1,064 or 0.01 percent were American Indians, and 147,613 or 89.61 percent were Whites. That is, only 10.39 percent of the administrators were people of color. A similar pattern of underrepresentation is present in the two databases employed for this chapter (Table 1).

TABLE 1
Percentage Distribution of Full-Time Administrative Positions by Database: Fall 1998

	Database	
Race/Ethnicity	NSOPF:99	NASPA:99
Black/African American, Non-Hispanic	6.5	8.6
Hispanic	2.6	2.7
Asian/Pacific Islander	2.7	1.0
American Indian/Alaska Native	0.6	0.6
White, Non-Hispanic	87.6	87.6

Note: Percentages may not add to 100 because of rounding.
Sources: U.S. Department of Education, 2002; National Study of Postsecondary Faculty: 1999; National Association of Student Personnel Administrators Salary Survey, 1999.

Academic Leaders

The gender gap in academic leadership positions was pronounced in favor of males (63.1 percent to 36.9 percent—Table 2). For Blacks/African Americans this pattern was reversed; however, Blacks/African American women out-numbered Blacks/African American males in academic leadership positions by 5.6 percentage points (47.2 percent males versus 52.8 percent females). Blacks/African Americans were the only group where the gender gap was reversed in favor of females. When examining the highest degree attained, Whites were more likely to have a bachelor's degree or less than people of color.

Overall, the average age of academic leaders was 51.7 (Table 3). The largest portion of people of color in academic leadership positions fell in the age category of 45 to 55 (48 percent), with no other age category close in

TABLE 2

Percentage of Distribution of Full-Time Academic Leaders by Gender, Highest Educational Credential Attained, and Race or Ethnicity: Fall 1998

Race/Ethnicity	Gender		Highest Credential Attained		
	Male	Female	Doctorate Degree	Master/First Degree	Bachelor's Professional or Less
All Races/Ethnicities	63.1	36.9	55.3	37.7	7.0
Black/African American, Non-Hispanic	47.2	52.8	54.3	43.6	2.1
Hispanic	64.1	35.9	38.0	54.8	7.2
Asian/Pacific Islander	55.2	44.8	47.7	47.7	4.9
American Indian/ Alaska Native	*	*	*	*	*
White, Non-Hispanic	64.6	35.4	56.1	36.5	7.3

*Sample too small.
Note: Percentages may not add to 100 because of rounding.
Sources: U.S. Department of Education, National Center for Education Statistics, 2002; National Study of Postsecondary Faculty: 1999.

TABLE 3

Average Age and Percentage Distribution of Full-Time Academic Leaders by Race or Ethnicity: Fall 1998

Race/ Ethnicity	Average Age	Percentage in Each Category					
		Under 35	35–44	45–55	54–64	65–70	71 or Older
All Races/ Ethnicities	51.7	5.5	14.6	39.5	33.9	4.7	1.8
Black/African American, Non-Hispanic	50.7	6.7	16.3	48.3	18.3	8.0	2.5
Hispanic	46.2	23.0	13.9	38.6	19.5	2.4	2.5
Asian/Pacific Islander	50.1	3.0	28.5	32.4	31.5	4.7	0.0
American Indian/Alaska Native	*	*	*	*	*	*	*
White, Non-Hispanic	52.0	5.0	13.9	39.1	35.6	4.6	1.8

*Sample too small.
Note: Percentages may not add to 100 because of rounding.
Sources: U.S. Department of Education, National Center for Education Statistics, 2002; National Study of Postsecondary Faculty: 1999.

representation. This finding seems to signal a pipeline challenge for institutions regarding ethnic and racial diversity in administrative positions. That is, it appears that institutions made significant efforts to recruit and retain this age cohort, but that no such effort has followed to replace those nearing retirement. Interestingly, it seems that people of color in academic leadership positions work to an older age than their White counterparts. Nonetheless, the average age distribution and representation in age cohorts suggest that overall growth of ethnic and racial diversity in the higher education administrative workforce will be a significant challenge over the next thirty years.

On balance, the mix of principal work activities varied across race and ethnicity groups (Table 4). American Indians/Alaska Natives spent more of their

TABLE 4

Percentage Distribution of Full-Time Instructional Faculty and Staff by Time Spent on Various Activities and Race or Ethnicity: Fall 1998

	Principal Activity			
Race/Ethnicity	Teaching Activities	Research Activities	Administrative Activities	Other Activities*
All Races/Ethnicities	64.5	11.3	12.8	11.4
Black/African American, Non-Hispanic	67.5	4.0	16.1	12.3
Hispanic	64.9	13.2	9.9	11.9
Asian/Pacific Islander	50.8	27.5	5.5	16.3
American Indian/ Alaska Native	73.2	9.5	10.3	7.0
White, Non-Hispanic	65.3	10.4	13.3	11.0

*Includes clinical services, sabbatical from this institution, technical activities, other institutional activities such as library services, community public service, subsidized performer, and artist in residence.
Note: Percentages may not add to 100 because of rounding.
Sources: U.S. Department of Education, National Center for Education Statistics, 2002; National Study of Postsecondary Faculty: 1999.

time (73.2 percent) and Asians/Pacific Islanders less of their time (50.8 percent) on teaching activities than other groups (overall average of 64.5 percent). Blacks/African Americans participated in research activities far less (4.0 percent) than other groups, while Asians/Pacific Islanders participated more (27.5 percent). Blacks/African Americans also participated in administrative activities more than the other groups (16.1 percent), while Asians/Pacific Islanders participated less (5.5 percent). Participation in "other activities" was fairly balanced for all groups, except for the low participation of American Indians/Alaska Natives (7.0 percent).

The distribution of academic leaders by rank showed variation by group (Table 5). The highest proportion of full professors was White (39.0 percent) or Asian/Pacific Islander (31.6 percent), compared with Blacks/African Americans, for whom the highest proportion was associate professors (26.8 percent).

TABLE 5

Percentage Distribution of Full-Time Academic Leaders by Academic Rank and Race or Ethnicity: Fall 1998

	Academic Rank				
Race/Ethnicity	Full Professor	Associate Professor	Assistant Professor	Instructor or Lecturer	Other Ranks/ Not Applicable
All Races/ Ethnicities	36.8	19.7	7.8	13.4	22.3
Black/African American, Non-Hispanic	18.9	26.8	16.0	14.4	23.9
Hispanic	17.1	21.1	5.3	22.3	34.2
Asian/Pacific Islander	31.6	26.2	5.5	5.7	31.0
American Indian/ Alaska Native	*	*	*	*	*
White, Non-Hispanic	39.0	19.0	7.2	13.3	21.5

*Sample too small.

Note: Percentages may not add to 100 because of rounding.

Sources: U.S. Department of Education, National Center for Education Statistics, 2002; National Study of Postsecondary Faculty: 1999.

Last, the highest proportion for Hispanics (34.2 percent) was "other ranks/not applicable."

Average income for academic leaders was examined for differences by source. For the most part, Whites had higher incomes in all source areas (Table 6). Asians/Pacific Islanders, however, had higher incomes with regard to total earned income ($75,319.10) and basic salary from institution ($71,458.60). All other ethnic and racial groups had salaries below the average for each source area.

Groups varied in their top two categories when looking at the distribution of academic leaders by program area (Table 7). The top two categories for Blacks/African Americans were education (27.3 percent) and "all other fields"

TABLE 6

Average Income of Full-Time Academic Leaders by Source of Income and Race or Ethnicity: Fall 1998

| Race/Ethnicity | Source of Income | | | | |
	Total Earned Income	Basic Salary from Institution	Other Income from Institution	Outside Consulting Income	Other Outside Income
All Races/ Ethnicities	71,617.80	67,680.20	9,560.50	7,840.10	7,127.40
Black/African American, Non-Hispanic	60,698.70	58,465.90	6,817.00	3,972.30	*
Hispanic	55,088.50	52,253.90	9,344.90	*	*
Asian/Pacific Islander	75,319.10	71,458.60	*	*	*
American Indian/ Alaska Native	*	*	*	*	*
White, Non-Hispanic	72,883.50	68,749.30	9,671.90	7,881.10	6,992.70

*Sample too small.
Note: Percentages may not add to 100 because of rounding.
Sources: U.S. Department of Education, National Center for Education Statistics, 2002; National Study of Postsecondary Faculty: 1999.

(16.4 percent); for Hispanics were education (25.9 percent) and humanities (17.9 percent); for Asians/Pacific Islanders were "all other fields" (20.4 percent) and engineering (17.4 percent); and for Whites were "all other fields" (18.2 percent) and humanities (15.1 percent). For the most part, people of color were largely concentrated in program areas deemed to be "caring fields" (home economics, education, health sciences, and social sciences).

An examination of employment status by Carnegie classification showed that, for the most part, people of color were represented variously across classification categories in academic leadership positions (Table 8). Asians/Pacific Islanders were better represented at research institutions (52.2 percent), Hispanics at doctoral institutions (14.3 percent), and Blacks/African Americans

TABLE 7

Percentage Distribution of Full-Time Academic Leaders by Race or Ethnicity and Degree Program Area: Fall 1998

	All Races/ Ethnicities	Race/Ethnicity				
		Black/African American, Non-Hispanic	Hispanic	Asian/Pacific Islander	American Indian/ Alaska Native	White, Non-Hispanic
Agriculture/ Home Economics	1.8	1.8	1.4	0.0	*	1.9
Business	5.6	1.8	4.4	4.7	*	6.0
Education	12.9	27.3	25.9	7.2	*	11.7
Engineering	4.2	4.0	4.5	17.4	*	3.6
Fine Arts	4.7	1.1	5.8	7.0	*	4.8
Health Sciences	13.1	15.6	10.6	7.7	*	13.3
Humanities	14.5	11.9	17.9	2.8	*	15.1
Natural Sciences	13.8	5.6	6.4	18.1	*	14.4
Social Sciences	11.4	14.6	14.1	14.7	*	10.9
All Other Fields	17.9	16.4	9.1	20.4	*	18.2

* Sample too small.

Note: Percentages may not add to 100 because of rounding.

Sources: U.S. Department of Education, National Center for Education Statistics, 2002; National Study of Postsecondary Faculty: 1999.

TABLE 8
Percentage Distribution of Full-Time Academic Leaders by Carnegie Classification and Race or Ethnicity: Fall 1998

	Carnegie Classification			
Race/Ethnicity	Research Institutions	Doctoral Institutions	Comprehensive Institutions	Liberal Arts Institutions
All Races/Ethnicities	39.8	15.7	28.4	16.2
Black/African American, Non-Hispanic	30.2	9.3	29.5	30.9
Hispanic	38.8	14.3	39.1	7.8
Asian/Pacific Islander	52.2	8.5	29.3	10.0
American Indian/ Alaska Native	*	*	*	*
White, Non-Hispanic	40.1	16.4	28.1	15.5

*Sample too small.
Note: Percentages may not add to 100 because of rounding.
Sources: U.S. Department of Education, National Center for Education Statistics, 2002; National Study of Postsecondary Faculty: 1999.

at liberal arts institutions (30.9 percent), although research institutions were a close second (30.2 percent). Overall, however, people of color were best represented at comprehensive institutions (29.5 percent for Blacks/African Americans, 39.1 percent for Hispanics, and 29.3 percent for American Indians/Alaska Natives).

As it relates to institutional control (Table 9), the largest percentage of the workforce was at public (66.2 percent) opposed to private (33.8 percent) institutions. Asians/Pacific Islanders were slightly better represented at public institutions with 79.7 percent, while Blacks/African Americans (38.8 percent) and Hispanics (41.9 percent) were slightly better represented at private institutions. As for institutional type (four-year versus two-year), the largest percentage of the workforce was at four-year (86.3 percent) institutions. Hispanics (21.9 percent) and Asians/Pacific Islanders (30.1 percent) were better represented at two-year institutions.

TABLE 9

Percentage of Distribution of Full-Time Academic Leaders by Institutional Control and Type and Race or Ethnicity: Fall 1998

Race/Ethnicity	Institutional Control		Institutional Type	
	Public	Private	4-Year	2-Year
All Races/Ethnicities	66.2	33.8	86.3	13.7
Black/African American, Non-Hispanic	61.2	38.8	80.9	19.1
Hispanic	58.1	41.9	78.1	21.9
Asian/Pacific Islander	79.7	20.3	69.9	30.1
American Indian/ Alaska Native	*	*	*	*
White, Non-Hispanic	66.3	33.7	87.5	12.5

*Sample too small.
Note: Percentages may not add to 100 because of rounding.
Sources: U.S. Department of Education, National Center for Education Statistics, 2002; National Study of Postsecondary Faculty: 1999.

An analysis of employment by region revealed that people of color are more likely to work at institutions in regions with a higher proportion of their group represented in the general population (Table 10). For example, the largest percentage of Blacks/African Americans and Hispanics was located in the Southeast, and the largest percentage of Asians/Pacific Islanders in the Far West.

A key aspect of the selection process for academic leaders is their performance as faculty; two indicators used for evaluation are publications and presentations (Trix and Psenka, 2003) (Table 11). The coin of the realm in academe is refereed publications. An evaluation of the average number of career publications and presentations revealed lower numbers, in general, and significantly lower numbers in specific categories for Blacks/African Americans. African Americans had the lowest number, with 10.4 refereed career publications. Hispanics had the lowest number of nonrefereed publications, 8.7. As for total career books, monographs, and reports, Blacks/African Americans had 7.0. Both Blacks/African Americans (49.4) and Hispanics (58.3) had career presentations and exhibits averages well below those of other groups.

TABLE 10

Percentage Distribution of Full-Time Academic Leaders by Race or Ethnicity and Region: Fall 1998

	All Races/ Ethnicities	Black/African American, Non-Hispanic	Hispanic	Asian/Pacific Islander	American Indian/ Alaska Native	White, Non-Hispanic
				Race/Ethnicity		
New England	5.3	5.5	9.9	3.0	*	5.2
Mideast	13.1	16.0	12.1	11.9	*	13.0
Great Lakes	16.8	13.8	9.6	13.4	*	17.2
Plains	9.3	1.7	5.9	3.8	*	10.2
Southeast	26.2	43.9	26.3	10.6	*	25.3
Southwest	9.9	5.6	20.4	14.5	*	9.8
Rocky Mountains	5.7	1.0	2.9	2.0	*	6.2
Far West	13.9	12.4	13.0	40.8	*	13.1

*Sample too small.

Note: Percentages may not add to 100 because of rounding.

Sources: U.S. Department of Education, National Center for Education Statistics, 2002; National Study of Postsecondary Faculty: 1999.

TABLE 11
Average Number of Publications and Presentations in Career for Academic Leaders by Race or Ethnicity: Fall 1998

| | Publications and Presentations | | | |
Race/Ethnicity	Refereed Publications	Non-refereed Publications	Books, Monographs, and Reports	Presentations and Exhibits
All Races/ Ethnicities	24.4	18.5	9.8	62.8
Black/African American, Non-Hispanic	10.4	11.9	7.0	49.4
Hispanic	20.8	8.7	*	58.3
Asian/Pacific Islander	35.1	*	*	80.6
American Indian/ Alaska Native	*	*	*	*
White, Non-Hispanic	25.1	19.3	10.0	63.2

*Sample too small.
Note: Percentages may not add to 100 because of rounding.
Sources: U.S. Department of Education, National Center for Education Statistics, 2002; National Study of Postsecondary Faculty: 1999.

Student Affairs Administrators

An examination of the gender of all race or ethnicity groups for student affairs administrators revealed nearly a balance between males and females (50.8 percent versus 49.2 percent) (Table 12). Gender for student affairs administrators of color, however, showed a reverse gender gap: females outnumbered males for all groups except Whites. These data may document the official start of the "feminization" of the student affairs professions. As for the highest degree attained, people of color had a slightly higher percentage distribution of doctorate and master's degrees, compared with their White counterparts. Likewise, people of color had a modestly higher percentage of master's and first professional degrees in comparison with Whites. Fewer people of color in student

TABLE 12

Percentage Distribution of Full-Time Student Affairs Administrators by Gender, Highest Educational Credential Attained, and Race or Ethnicity: Fall 1998

| | Gender | | Highest Credential Attained | | |
Race/Ethnicity	Male	Female	Doctorate Degree	Master/First Degree	Bachelor's Professional or Less
All Races/Ethnicities	50.8	49.2	26.8	53.5	19.7
Black/African American, Non-Hispanic	44.5	54.5	31.1	63.6	15.2
Hispanic	45.8	54.2	23.2	60.0	16.8
Asian/Pacific Islander	39.4	60.6	20.0	62.9	17.2
American Indian/ Alaska Native	39.1	60.9	23.8	66.7	9.5
White, Non-Hispanic	51.8	48.2	26.6	53.1	20.3
Other	47.1	52.9	23.5	52.9	23.5

Note: Percentages may not add to 100 because of rounding.
Source: National Association of Student Personnel Administrators Salary Survey, 1999.

affairs administrative positions had only a bachelor's degree or less compared with Whites.

Looking at institution size (Table 13), Blacks/African Americans (24.1 percent) and Hispanics (27.4 percent) were most likely to be at institutions with 10,000 to 19,999 students, Asians/Pacific Islanders (31.4 percent) and American Indians/Alaska Natives (34.8 percent) at schools with 2,500 to 9,999 students, Whites and non-Hispanics (22.9 percent) at institutions with 1,000 to 2,499 students, and "others" (41.2 percent) at institutions with 5,000 to 9,999 students.

An analysis of income for student affairs administrators revealed results different from those found for their counterparts (Table 13). Whites had the lowest total earned income of all ethnic and racial groups ($71,614.70), Asians/Pacific Islanders the highest ($90,262.80), followed by Blacks/African Americans ($84,587.10) and Hispanics ($77,643.40).

TABLE 13

Percentage Distribution of Full-Time Student Affairs Administrators by Institutional Size, Average Income, and Race or Ethnicity: Fall 1998

Race/Ethnicity	Percentage in Each Category							Average Income
	Under 1,000	$1,000– 2,499	$2,500– 4,999	$5,000– 9,999	$10,000– 19,999	$20,000– 30,000	Over $30,000	Total Earned Income
All Races/Ethnicities	6.4	22.3	17.0	18.5	20.4	8.9	6.6	73,427.80
Black/African American, Non-Hispanic	4.3	18.0	16.4	11.0	24.1	14.0	12.0	84,587.10
Hispanic	6.3	18.9	11.6	11.6	27.4	11.6	12.6	77,643.40
Asian/Pacific Islander	2.9	22.9	31.4	8.6	17.1	5.7	11.4	90,262.80
American Indian/ Alaska Native	4.3	8.7	34.8	34.8	13.0	4.3	0.0	*
White, Non-Hispanic	6.7	22.9	16.9	19.3	19.9	8.4	5.9	71,614.70
Other	0.0	17.6	23.5	41.2	11.8	0.0	5.9	*

*Sample too small.

Note: Percentages may not add to 100 because of rounding.

Source: National Association of Student Personnel Administrators Salary Survey, 1999.

The distribution of student affairs administrators by institutional type and control provides a perspective on the kinds of institutions at which these administrators were employed (Table 14). When considering institutional type (two-year, four-year, and university),[3] Blacks/African Americans and non-Hispanics (11.7 percent) and Asians/Pacific Islanders (8.6 percent) had the highest representation. At four-year colleges, American Indians/Alaska Natives (56.5 percent) and Asians/Pacific Islanders (42.9 percent) had the highest representation. At universities, Hispanics (75.8 percent) and "others" (64.7 percent) had the highest representation. At public institutions, American Indians/Alaska Natives (78.3 percent) and "others" (76.5 percent) had the highest representation, while at private institutions, Whites (39.0 percent) and Hispanics (36.5 percent) had the highest representation.

Like that for academic leaders, an analysis of student affairs employment by region reveals that people of color generally work at institutions in regions that

Table 14
Percentage of Distribution of Full-Time Student Affairs Administrators, by Institutional Type and Institutional Control, and by Race or Ethnicity: Fall 1998

	Institutional Type			Institutional Control	
Race/Ethnicity	2-Year	4-Year	University	Public	Private College
All Races/Ethnicities	7.7	37.4	54.9	62.1	37.9
Black/African American, non-Hispanic	11.7	26.7	61.6	71.4	28.6
Hispanic	3.2	21.1	75.8	63.5	36.5
Asian/Pacific Islander	8.6	42.9	48.6	65.7	34.3
American Indian/ Alaskan Native	0.0	56.5	43.5	78.3	21.7
White, non-Hispanic	7.5	38.8	53.7	61.0	39.0
Other*	5.9	29.4	64.7	76.5	23.5

* "Other" consisted of professional degrees, associate degrees, and certificates.
Note: Percentages may not sum to 100 due to rounding.
Source: National Association for Student Personnel Administrators (NASPA) Salary Survey, 1999.

FIGURE 2
NASPA Regions

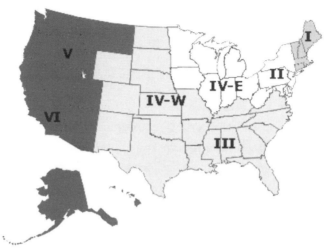

Source: National Association for Student Administrators (NASPA) Web site, http://www.naspa.org/regions/default.cfm.

have similar groups in the general population (Figure 2, Table 15). For example, the largest percentage of Blacks/African Americans and Hispanics was located in Region III, the largest percentage of Asians/Pacific Islanders in Region VI, and the largest percentage of American Indians/Alaska Natives in Region V.

The analysis by position type showed great variation by race or ethnicity (Table 16). In single-position categories, the highest percentage of Blacks/African Americans (14.0 percent) were senior student affairs officers, Hispanics (12.4 percent) were directors of career counseling, Asians/Pacific Islanders (14.3 percent) were associate deans of students, American Indians/Alaska Natives were associate deans of students or directors of the student union (13.0 percent), Whites (11.2 percent) were senior student affairs officers, and "others" (17.6 percent) were associate deans of students.

Conclusion

This chapter provides an analysis of the administrative workforce in higher education with a focus on racial or ethnic diversity. It is timely and significant because the demographic breakdown presented fills an important void in knowledge. Work activities by race or ethnicity exhibit important variations.

TABLE 15

Percentage Distribution of Full-Time Student Affairs Administrators by Race or Ethnicity and Region: Fall 1998

	All Races/Ethnicities	Black/African American, Non-Hispanic	Hispanic	Asian/Pacific Islander	American Indian/ Alaska Native	White, Non-Hispanic	Other*
				Race/Ethnicity			
Region I	8.9	6.4	4.6	11.8	0.0	9.3	12.5
Region II	16.0	16.3	11.5	5.9	21.7	16.3	6.3
Region III	24.8	32.0	32.2	0.0	13.0	24.3	12.5
Region IV-E	21.6	20.7	18.4	2.9	13.0	22.1	12.5
Region IV-W	15.6	13.9	16.1	11.8	17.4	15.8	0.0
Region V	6.9	3.0	2.3	14.7	30.4	7.2	6.3
Region VI	6.2	7.5	14.9	52.9	4.3	5.0	50.0

* "Other" consisted of professional degrees, associate degrees, and certificates.

Note: Percentages may not add to 100 because of rounding.

Source: National Association of Student Personnel Administrators Salary Survey, 1999.

TABLE 16

Percentage Distribution of Full-Time Student Affairs Administrators by Race or Ethnicity and Position: Fall 1998

				Race/Ethnicity			
Position	All Races/ Ethnicities	Black/African American, Non-Hispanic	Hispanic	Asian/Pacific Islander	American Indian/ Alaska Native	White, Non-Hispanic	Other
Senior Student Affairs Officer	11.4	14.0	10.3	11.4	4.3	11.2	5.9
Associate Senior Student Affairs Officer	4.0	7.1	4.1	8.6	4.3	3.6	0.0
Assistant Senior Student Affairs Officer	4.4	6.2	5.2	0.0	4.3	4.3	0.0
Dean of Students	4.4	7.5	7.2	0.0	8.7	4.1	0.0
Associate Dean of Students	3.6	5.5	5.2	14.3	13.0	3.1	17.6
Assistant Dean of Students	4.1	11.0	5.2	8.6	4.3	3.3	5.9
Counseling Center	9.4	9.1	6.2	8.6	4.3	9.5	11.8
Financial Aid	7.1	4.5	9.3	0.0	8.7	7.3	11.8
Career Counseling	9.2	5.8	12.4	11.4	8.7	9.4	0.0
Health Center	8.3	4.9	3.1	8.6	8.7	8.8	11.8
Student Union	6.7	7.5	6.2	5.7	13.0	6.6	5.9
Security	6.5	4.9	2.1	2.9	8.7	6.7	11.8
Admissions	6.8	4.5	6.2	5.7	4.3	7.1	5.9
Registration	5.3	0.6	6.2	2.9	0.0	5.7	5.9
Housing	8.9	6.8	11.3	11.4	4.3	9.0	5.9

Note: Percentages may not add to 100 because of rounding.

Source: National Association of Student Personnel Administrators Salary Survey, 1999.

FIGURE 3
Minority Group Representation in the United States

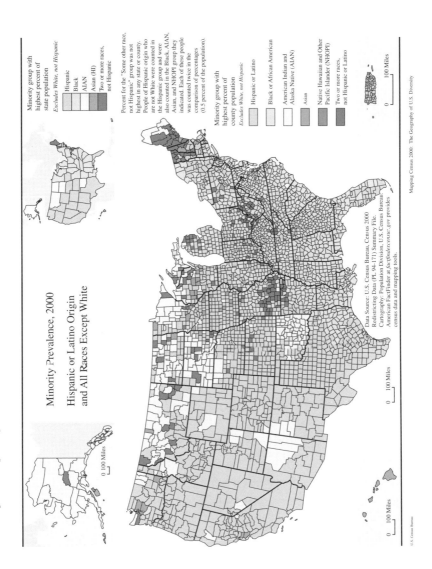

Minority Prevalence, 2000

Hispanic or Latino Origin
and All Races Except White

Minority group with
highest percent of
state population
Excludes White, not Hispanic

- Hispanic
- Black
- AIAN
- Asian (HI)
- Two or more races,
  not Hispanic

Percent for the "Some other race,
not Hispanic" group was not
highest in any state or county.
People of Hispanic origin who
are not White were counted in
the Hispanic group and were
also counted in the Black, AIAN,
Asian, and NHOPI group they
indicated. Each of these people
was counted twice in the
comparison of percentages
(0.5 percent of the population).

Minority group with
highest percent of
county population
Excludes White, not Hispanic

- Hispanic or Latino
- Black or African American
- American Indian and
  Alaska Native (AIAN)
- Asian
- Native Hawaiian and Other
  Pacific Islander (NHOPI)
- Two or more races,
  not Hispanic or Latino

0 ___ 100 Miles

Data Source: U.S. Census Bureau, Census 2000
Redistricting Data (PL 94-171) Summary File.
Cartography: Population Division, U.S. Census Bureau.
American FactFinder at *factfinder.census.gov* provides
census data and mapping tools.

Mapping Census 2000: The Geography of U.S. Diversity

U.S. Census Bureau

Asians/Pacific Islanders emphasized research, which is likely linked to the previously identified higher salaries and promotion rates; Blacks/African Americans emphasized administration, which is likely linked to their lower research production, promotion, and tenure rates; and American Indians/Alaska Natives emphasized teaching, which is likely linked to their previously reported absence in administration (Lynch and Charleston, 1990; Warner, 1995).

Two pipeline challenges emerged from the analysis of national data on the administrative workforce for people of color. For the most part, people of color assume administrative positions sooner than their White counterparts. This situation is particularly challenging for academic leaders because it impedes progress through the professorial ranks and decreases research productivity, which are both likely linked to not achieving senior-level positions. Next, important gaps in age cohorts are apparent, which may best be understood in three waves (see Table 3). The first wave of people of color to assume positions in higher education, the largest one, is nearing retirement age. The second wave represents an opportunity lost because institutions did not hire at the same rate; thus, the momentum of integration seen in the first wave has not been sustained. The third and current wave is not as large as the first wave, but it shows improvement over the second wave. Interestingly, this wave is showing a spike in participation by Hispanics.

Data from our analyses show a reversed gender gap for people of color in administrative positions. Although males overall continue to hold a larger percentage of both academic leader and student affairs positions, this trend does not hold true when taking race and ethnicity into account. For Blacks/African Americans, females are more likely to hold both academic leader and student affairs positions. For student affairs positions, all racial and ethnic minority groups show majority females, unlike for Whites.

Location matters for people of color in administrative positions in higher education. For the most part, administrators of color are employed at comprehensive and liberal arts institutions and are largely concentrated at four-year public institutions. Administrators of color are most represented at institutions located in regions of the country with the largest populations of their specific group (Figure 3). Blacks/African Americans, for example, are located in the Southeast, and Asians/Pacific Islanders in the Far West.

Barriers Encountered by Administrators of Color in Higher and Postsecondary Education

BARRIERS FACING PEOPLE OF COLOR in administrative positions in higher and postsecondary education come in a variety of forms and affect not only experiences in the workplace (L. Benjamin, 1997; Jackson, 2003a, 2004b) but also interpersonal attitudes and perceptions of self-efficacy (Abney and Richey, 1991; Howard-Hamilton and Williams, 1996). This chapter highlights and describes many barriers previously identified in the research literature in an effort to understand the scope of challenges related to diversifying the administrative workforce in higher and postsecondary education. It is not a synthesis or reconceptualization of barriers but a consolidation of published research on the challenges facing aspiring administrators of color. A description of barriers assists key decision makers at institutions of higher education in developing appropriate programs and initiatives to address and ultimately remove persistent barriers. Additionally, a discussion of barriers illuminates some historical challenges facing efforts to diversify the workforce and allows individuals to evaluate whether current efforts to remove barriers are successful.

Three main questions drive the following discussion: (1) What conceptual and legal frameworks are most helpful in understanding issues of underrepresentation in the administrative workforce? (2) What are the professional barriers facing administrators of color in higher and postsecondary education? (3) Do female administrators of color face unique barriers? Accordingly, this chapter is organized in three main sections to address these three complex questions. The first section describes the various approaches and frameworks used to identify, explain, and remedy underrepresentation for people of color in the U.S. workforce. The next section describes the barriers that affect individual career trajectories: social barriers; institutional or organizational barriers; and internal barriers. The final section describes career barriers specific to female administrators of color. Although women of color share challenges related to racial discrimination with their male counterparts, they also experience additional barriers because of their gender.

Legal and Conceptual Frameworks

The higher education literature contains multiple frameworks in the form of concepts, theories, and models that have been advanced to identify and describe the underrepresentation of people of color in administrative and leadership positions (executive or senior leadership). Nestled among other larger theoretical perspectives on race (critical race theory and LatCrit) and gender (feminist theory) in society are a few that speak specifically to diversification in an employment setting. As the current text is primarily concerned with the challenges and successes in diversifying the workforce, readers are directed to other resources for a thorough discussion of these larger theoretical perspectives. Among the most critical and useful frameworks for understanding the historical considerations of race, gender, and the U.S. workforce are affirmative action, disparate impact theory, underutilization analysis, representative bureaucracy theory, and the glass ceiling (Exhibit 1).

The concept of affirmative action was first introduced into the national discourse by President Kennedy in the early 1960s (Executive Order No. 10925, 13 C.F.R., 1960). Since then it has become widely understood that affirmative action is defined by proactive programs and strategies designed to provide opportunities for women, people of color, and other marginalized groups in employment, education, and business (U.S. Commission on Civil Rights, 1995). Historically and more recently, racial bias and discrimination in institutions of higher education have come under scrutiny in the courts (Jackson, 2004c; Weinberg, 2008). For example, the U.S. Supreme Court decisions *University of California* v. *Bakke* (1978) and *Grutter* v. *Bollinger* (2003), while underscoring different rationales, both affirmed the importance of diversity in higher education. The goal of affirmative action is not to advantage people of color or disadvantage Whites but to give equal opportunities

EXHIBIT 1
Legal and Conceptual Frameworks for Understanding Underrepresentation in the Administrative Workforce

Name	Type of Framework	
Affirmative Action	Legal and Social	Most closely associated with racial equity, affirmative action refers to programs and policies to address the effects of prior discriminatory acts through programs and policies designed to promote diversity and equal opportunity for underrepresented groups of individuals.
Disparate Impact Theory	Legal	Situated in labor and employment law, disparate impact theory describes the adverse impact nominally unbiased employment practices have on protected classes of citizens. If an adverse impact is demonstrated, continuing the employment practice without demonstrating the business necessity of the practice may constitute unlawful discrimination.
Underutilization Analysis	Conceptual	Underutilization analysis is a method for assessing inequality. The basic tenet is a comparison of the representation of individuals from marginalized groups in a particular setting to the representation of that same group in society at large.
Representative Bureaucracy Theory	Conceptual	The theory of representative bureaucracy suggests that organizations perform better when leaders and decision makers reflect the characteristics of their constituents.
The Glass Ceiling	Conceptual	The glass ceiling describes a set of invisible and impermeable barriers that prevent underrepresented groups from ascending to positions of power and leadership.

and access to government-funded initiatives (civil service and state universities) (Jackson, 2003a; Kaplin and Lee, 1995). Therefore, for colleges and universities, it was deemed appropriate to consider race as a viable criterion along with the many other criteria used to make hiring and admissions decisions (Jackson, 2003a). As data on the higher education workforce currently demonstrate, however, racial and ethnic diversity on our campuses has yet to be fully achieved (see the previous chapter).

Disparate impact theory is arguably one of the most important developments in antidiscrimination and employment law (Selmi, 2006) and has been successfully applied in higher education research (Jackson, 2006a; Kidder and Rossner, 2002; O'Callaghan, 2007; Perez, 2004). Common elements of a class action suit in the employment context include alleged systemic discrimination, statistical proof of discrimination, a challenge to the legitimacy of the employer's statistical proof, and an assertion of the business necessity for the disputed practice or policy (Employment Discrimination Coordinator, 2005). For disparate impact claims, the burden of proof always rests with the employee.

An important distinction to make is *disparate impact* and *disparate treatment* claims. Although both claims arise in the context of discrimination cases, disparate treatment occurs when an employer intended to treat a member of a protected class[4] in a way that is substantially different from other individuals based on particular characteristics of the individual (race or gender). Disparate impact does not require the plaintiff to demonstrate that the employer actually intended to discriminate against members of a protected class. Rather, it is enough that a seemingly neutral employment practice or policy has an adverse impact on a protected class of individuals.

As a conceptual and theoretical framework, underutilization analysis has recently been discussed in the scholarly and practice-based literature as a way of unpacking diversity data in institutions of higher education (Weinberg, 2008). As a new analytic approach to measuring levels of faculty diversity, underutilization analysis closely follows what the federal government has termed "utilization analyses." In measuring the underuse of marginalized groups in higher education, underutilization calls for comparisons between the expected number of minority faculty in an academic department with the actual number of minority faculty available on a national level. The expected values are calculated based on employment data available from national sources (trade associations and professional licensing bodies). More specifically, this approach demands attention to two levels of diversity: the diversity present in a given institution and the expected level of diversity in a given disciplinary area based on national employment trend data. For example, underutilization analysis suggests that the level of racial and ethnic diversity present in a particular academic department should be compared against the levels of racial and ethnic diversity present in the workforce in that academic area on a national basis. The power of this "granular approach" is its ability to unmask general claims that institutions are diverse by virtue of increasing numbers of faculty of color on campus (Weinberg, 2008). This approach has the ability to reveal academic areas where high, or higher, concentrations of faculty of color are present and to critique other areas where few or no faculty of color are present.

In both the higher education and public administration literature (Flowers, 2003; Jackson, 2004b; Meier and Stewart, 1992), the theory of representative bureaucracy posits that institutions and organizations function better and more efficiently if the characteristics of decision makers accurately reflect those of their constituents. Additionally, it is presumed that decisions made by the leadership groups in fact respond to the concerns of the constituents (Meier and Nigro, 1976). This framework has been used in the study of higher education to underscore the importance of having leaders in higher education who reflect the demographic composition of students (Flowers, 2003; Jackson, 2004c). The logic that underscores this framework as it relates to administrators of color is clearly illustrated in Figure 1, Three-Tiered Approach to Institutional Diverstiy: college and university administrators maintain power and control over subordinate groups in the institution (faculty and students). Assuming that administrators take a professional oath to serve faculty and students, representative bureaucracy suggests that the more diverse a leadership group, the more accurately it will respond to the multitude concerns presented by an increasingly diverse institution.

The concept of glass ceiling has been used to describe a myriad of barriers (including social and institutional) to career advancement for women and people of color. Since the 1980s, the federal government has recognized the existence of a glass ceiling that prohibits the advancement of women and people of color in the workplace. In 1987, the Department of Labor published a report, *Workforce 2000,* which brought widespread attention to the composition of the U.S. workforce, including the increased importance of men and women of all races as major contributors to the American economy. To investigate and remedy exposed inequities in the workplace, a bipartisan commission was created through Title II of the Civil Rights Act of 1991 (Jackson and O'Callaghan, 2009).

Part of what makes the glass ceiling framework so compelling is its ability to capture the public consciousness yet simultaneously define a specific form of discrimination that can be measured in educational research. In an attempt to place parameters around this amorphous concept, four employment-based criteria have been proposed to identify discrimination resulting from the glass ceiling. From the field of sociology, Cotter, Hermsen, Ovadia, and Vanneman (2001) assert four specific criteria that define and describe a glass ceiling: (1) a gender or racial difference that is not explained by other job-relevant characteristics of the employee; (2) a gender or racial difference that is greater at higher levels of an institution than at lower levels; (3) a gender or racial inequality in the chances of advancement into higher levels, not merely the proportion of each gender or race currently at those higher levels; and (4) a gender or racial inequality that increases over the course of a career. Cotter, Hermsen, Ovadia, and Vanneman (2001) tested this concept with regard to earnings, and Maume (2004) subsequently tested it for managerial attainment, but the theory has heretofore not been applied to educational research. This area is ripe for future research.

In summary, the legal and conceptual frameworks for understanding underrepresentation in the academic workforce are useful tools for institutions in striving to alter and improve the working conditions for all employees, including administrators of color. Regardless of which framework an institution chooses to adopt in the development of programs or policies to increase levels of diversity, these frameworks all have at least one unifying theme: the inclusion of ethnic and racial diversity is of benefit to educational institutions and their leadership teams and should be promoted. Leaving the conceptual issues related to discrimination aside for the moment, we now turn our attention to specific barriers faced by administrators of color in higher education.

Established Barriers for Administrators of Color

One difficulty with the historical literature on barriers for administrators of color is the categorical nature in which racism and sexism were recognized and discussed. Current and future research efforts are beginning to see the intersections and overlaps between various sets of social categories and oppressions, and a call for research on this topic has arisen across disciplines. As it relates to the study of higher education, a possible direction for future research may seek to document the experiences—the successes and challenges—of administrators of color using intersectionality analysis (Crenshaw, 1991; McCall, 2005). This section, however, is dedicated to a discussion of barriers that have been previously identified and discussed in the research literature. As a result, concrete and basic distinctions based on prior research have been used to categorize the studies and findings outlined in the following paragraphs.

Barriers to success in a career for people of color are pervasive and not confined to a particular sector of the economy or to particular industries (Jackson and O'Callaghan, 2009). Rather, barriers appear to be universal in their impact and affect individuals of color regardless of where they choose to pursue careers. For example, Bell and Nkomo (2001) identified numerous barriers facing African American business executives. Eight-hour in-depth life history interviews with eighty African American women and forty White women executives and a survey of 825 African American and White women managers revealed a multitude of barriers to success in a career. Even though 75 percent of the sample worked in Fortune 500 companies, each woman confronted the role of her gender or race in the working world.

Regardless of the origin or location of barriers (or mechanisms by which they are perpetuated), the outcomes they produce are apparent on the landscape of higher education. They include underrepresentation in the upper and senior levels of administrative and decision-making positions (L. Benjamin, 1997; Jackson, 2003a, 2004b), employment in positions that are ill defined and lack authority (L. Benjamin, 1997), a concentration of people of color in stressful, low-paying, low-status jobs (Howard-Vital, 1987; Mosley, 1980; Wolfman, 1997), low satisfaction with work (Bell and Nkomo, 2001), and the belief that people of color are "token" hires (Watson, 2001). As the research points out, barriers stemming from social and institutional forces come in a variety of forms and are experienced in a multitude of ways. Lindsay (1994), for example, noted that stereotypes and prejudice, a negative institutional climate, structural policies and conditions that disadvantage people of color, and a lack of mentoring and networking for people of color are all factors that hinder the presence of African Americans (especially women) in pivotal decision-making roles in higher education.

In an attempt to understand the root causes of the current low representation of administrators of color, we now turn to a description of barriers identified in the research literature that they face in the higher education workforce. These barriers are divided into three sections: social, organizational and institutional, and internal (Figure 4; see also Jones [2000] for an alternative conceptualization of levels of racism). An easy way to conceive of barriers affecting individuals at each level is nesting. Individuals are affected not only by issues related directly to them (internal) but also by the issues affecting the institutions where they work (organizational and institutional) and the society in which those organizations exist (social). The individual is nested in an organization, and that organization is in turn nested in society. For example, an individual barrier to obtaining an executive-level leadership position might be lack of a terminal degree. An institutional or organizational barrier might be lack of access to a mentor able to provide the guidance necessary to obtain a high-level position. A social barrier could be the racial climate in which the institution is situated. In a city or region that is highly segregated, it might not be possible to obtain a position of leadership because of the discriminatory forces working against such a career trajectory.

Social Barriers

Social barriers to advancement for administrators of color include external social forces and pressures that permeate educational organizations (Green, 1997; Harvard, 1986; Watson, 2001). Organizations do not exist in a vacuum; they are run and managed by individuals who may exert prejudiced attitudes in the workplace. Some examples are sexism and racism, both of which have roots in larger sociohistorical mechanisms and value structures but find expression in the daily life and work of organizations (Green 1997; Harvard, 1986; Mosley, 1980; Watson, 2001). As noted by Green (1997), "Gender, race, power, and

FIGURE 4
Concentric Influence of Barriers for Administrators of Color

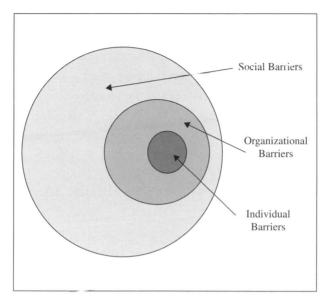

Social Barriers

Organizational
Barriers

Individual
Barriers

identity are inexorably intertwined in academia" (p. 147). Watson (2001) noted that "race and gender prevail as the two leading factors contributing to the discrimination [that] African-American women experience in the workplace" (p. 8). In particular, the social and external barriers that administrators of color face while working in higher education include general social attitudes (stereotypes) and prejudices about people of color (Coleman, 1998; Green, 1997; Howard-Hamilton and Williams, 1996; Watson, 2001).

While researching the special concerns of African American women in higher education, Mosley as early as 1980 documented social and institutional racism as the most dominant hindrances to achievement for people of color. The effects of racism in the workplace include the finding that administrators of color often have their views ignored and their authority and leadership challenged (Crase, 1994). Some of the effects of sexism include the prevalence of a singular male managerial model that continually emerges as the valued supervisory norm (Abney and Richey, 1991) and unequal pay.

Relying on a conceptual framework that highlights the centrality of race, gender, class, culture, and history, Bell and Nkomo (2001) note that "race still determines a woman's position within the labor market and her economic well-being. Race prevents minority women from fully participating in organizational life, with minority women managers reporting greater scrutiny and extra challenges because of their race" (p. 17). Accordingly, Bell and Nkomo found that African American women were less satisfied with their present positions than White women; moreover, a majority of the African American women noted they did not have significant decision-making duties, nor did they feel they were in positions that allowed them to exercise their skills and knowledge. Additionally, African American women felt they had to outperform their White colleagues to succeed and reported receiving less support from their managers and bosses. African American women also did not feel their companies had policies that would advance people of color. Bell and Nkomo (2001) noted six barriers experienced by their interviewees: daily doses of racism, being held to a higher standard than others, the "vice" of invisibility, exclusion from informal networks, challenges to authority, and hollow company commitments to the advancement of minorities.

Coleman (1998) used a survey to identify the individual, group, and organizational barriers to career advancement for female administrators in a variety of organizations ($n = 49$). Eighty-eight percent of African American women identified racial discrimination as the primary barrier to career advancement. In line with the recognition that racism and sexism are the two largest social barriers in the workplace, 79 percent of White women identified exclusion from the old boy network as the primary barrier.

In qualitative research with four African American females employed as midlevel administrators at a predominantly White, midsize public institution in the Midwest, Watson (2001) noted that the social context in which people of color interact forces a "constant awareness of cognitive processing when communicating with others" (p. 11). Essentially it requires continual attention to the ways in which nonverbal communications are perceived as well as managing responses to professional and interpersonal communications. Additionally, participants in Watson's small sample showed unanimous consensus when discussing issues of racial and gender discrimination against African

American women administrators and the effects of these forms of discrimination. The obstacles they face as administrators include their occupational status in higher education, the shared struggle with being accepted and treated as equals among colleagues, the existence of the "token syndrome," and the reality that higher education is a field dominated by White males.

It should be noted, however, that the centrality of race and its subsequent impact on working in higher education also affect African American males. According to Rolle, Davies, and Banning (2000), "Race is a major concept that structures the Black administrator in predominantly White institutions of higher education" (p. 89). Indeed, Rolle, Davies, and Banning effectively establish that race partially structures the administrative experience for African Americans; they note that many African American males are the first African Americans to hold their administrative position, African American males must constantly identify and cope with institutional racism (racist policies and organizational bias), they often seek to stretch the perceived identity of the African American administrator as working only for African American concerns on campus (affirmative action programming), and they must continually negotiate the physical differences that demarcate race in institutions such as skin color and language.

Organizational and Institutional Barriers

In contrast to the social forces that create barriers for people of color (both in and out of the workplace), specific organizational and institutional barriers can be directly linked to frustrating professional experiences for administrators of color (Figure 5). Rather than being recognized as racism or sexism on a grand scale, these barriers are often made manifest by policies, practices, and dicta influenced by greater social pressures. For example, in a society that values the leadership and contributions of a particular majority group, no policies may be in place to assist other minority groups in making inroads to leadership positions.

As they relate to higher education administration, many of the effects of institutional barriers have been identified in the literature as contributing to the underrepresentation of people of color in positions of senior or executive leadership. The effects include lack of access to professional networks for particular racial groups (Coleman, 1998; Crase, 1994; Martinez, 1999), a lack of

FIGURE 5
Relationship Between Organization and Individual

Organizational Barriers	+	Internal Barriers	=	Workplace Experiences

appropriate role models (Coleman, 1998; Crase, 1994), segregated networks of professionals (Braddock and McPartland, 1987), a lack of mentors for individuals of specific racial and ethnic groups (Crase, 1994), the lack of a post-graduate or terminal degree, the lack of fluency in a foreign language (Twombly, 1998), and work in academic departments or settings in which individuals are unwilling to reorganize their work or priorities around issues of cultural diversity (Crase, 1994). Lack of organizational fit and connectedness are also viewed as barriers for administrators of color (Howard-Hamilton and Williams, 1996).

Internal Barriers

A host of internal barriers facing administrators of color must be overcome to achieve their full potential as successful leaders in higher education (Abney and Richey, 1991; Mosley, 1980; Williams, 1986; Wolfman, 1997). Although the subject must be treated sensitively so that it is not interpreted as "blaming the victim," it must be noted that a host of literature (for example, Abney and Richey, 1991; Williams, 1986) written by and for administrators of color discusses this very topic and identifies specific interpersonal issues that must be addressed to achieve success. In addition, it might be useful to consult research from other disciplines (see Jones, 2000) on internalized racism to understand how societal messages about race may influence individual performance in the workplace.

These internal barriers include a fear of failure, low self-esteem, role conflict, fear of success, the perceived consequences of career advancement, and lack of an advanced degree, all of which may coalesce to prevent administrators of color from pursuing and achieving career advancement (Abney and Richey, 1991; Howard-Hamilton and Williams, 1996). Internal barriers appear to disproportionately affect women. In a study by Howard-Hamilton and Williams (1996), females viewed family responsibilities as a barrier to obtaining positions of leadership. Mosley (1980) also found the second most frequently mentioned hindrance to career success was the dual responsibility of combining a family and career. Wolfman (1997) identifies the "extended family ethnic," which describes the responsibilities many African American women have caring for three generations of family: grandparents, parents, and children. Wolfman also identifies church and community responsibilities as possibly contributing stress to balancing a career and personal life. Wolfman also goes on to note, however, that it is these same personal ties and responsibilities that give African American women relief from stress by providing "creative outlets and sources of renewal" (p. 164).

In recognition of the dual function that family and community may play in the careers of women, it is important to note a recent shift in the scholarly literature on this particular barrier—a balance between work and life. Rather than being a struggle that women must figure out on their own, educational institutions are beginning to recognize the singular role the academy can play in helping female faculty transform their family and personal obligations into assets rather than barriers in the workplace (Mason and Goulden, 2002, 2004a, 2004b; O'Callaghan, 2007; Thornton, 2005). The majority of research in this area, however, has been on female faculty, thus leaving scholarly research about balance in female administrators' worklife underresearched (see Hamilton [2002] for a portrait of successful African American female administrators and the decisions they faced along their career paths).

The "Double Burden": A Barrier Specific to Women of Color

Women of color in higher education administration face distinct barriers (see Berry and Mizelle, 2006, for recent scholarship on the experiences of female faculty of color). Terms such as "multiple jeopardy" (L. Benjamin, 1997; P. Benjamin, 1997; Chliwniak, 1997), "double jeopardy" (Irvine, 1978; Lindsay, 1994; Warner, 1995; Wilson, 1989), "triple jeopardy" (King, 1988; Lindsay, 1999), "double bind" (Warner, 1995), "dual burden" (Singh, Robinson, and Williams-Greene, 1995), "double solo" (Fontaine and Greenlee, 1993; Kanter, 1977), "interactive discrimination" (Irvine, 1978; Warner, 1995), and "racialized sexism" (Bell and Nkomo, 2001) appear frequently in the literature on women of color in higher education administration. These terms all describe the collective experience of navigating the conflicting expectations that arise when an individual is considered to have membership in two distinct marginalized groups (Dougherty, 1980; Warner, 1995), suffering the dual effects of racism and sexism.

According to Mosley (1980, p. 306), "Black female administrators have for many years held positions of leadership in Black academic institutions as founders, presidents, deans, and department chairpersons. In White academia, however, Black women administrators are, for the most part, invisible beings. Their status in higher education is a reflection of their status on the national scene—at the bottom." Although the forces of racism keep African American women from ascending to positions of power and authority in most areas of higher education, African American women have traditionally had greater opportunities at historically Black colleges and universities because of their emphasis on home economics, nursing, and teaching, where they formed a larger percentage of the faculty than males (Wilson, 1989). Additionally, it has been asserted that African American women's contributions to historically Black colleges and universities have provided stability for those institutions (Moore and Wagstaff, 1974), thus revealing another dual role in which African American women were able to access advanced educational opportunity and contribute to the formation of an entire educational industry focused on the empowerment and advancement of African Americans in society.

The positive role that historically Black colleges and universities have played in the advancement of African American female administrators notwithstanding, the effects of a double burden have been described as frustrating and discouraging. Indeed these effects can at times amplify a host of myths regarding job performance expectations, race, and gender (Watson, 2001). Although most often discussed in the context of African American female administrators, it should be noted that the double burden of race and sex is not limited to African Americans. Gorena (1996) notes that Hispanic women have also faced these two detrimental, overriding barriers to career advancement. In detailing their experiences, Gorena (1996) notes that Hispanic women also experience sex-based discrimination, receive less pay for comparable jobs than their male peers, receive the more undesirable job assignments, and remain in lower-status positions and jobs.

Approximately 92 percent of the sample from Fontaine and Greenlee's research (1993) indicated that African American women are doubly disadvantaged in their career advancement because of race and gender, and respondents agreed unanimously that women of color are "subjected to greater degrees of discrimination than are White women" (p. 123). As described by Lindsay (1994), the effects of being a woman of color in a male-dominated workplace is a catch-22: Women are often discriminated against when acting in accordance with male norms of management (acting aggressive and domineering) but are also denied advancement and employment opportunities for failing to be aggressive enough. Lindsay cites linguistic research showing that women must maintain a certain amount of deference in their speech lest they be assessed differently from men. If women spoke more than one-third of the time during meetings, they were viewed as domineering or overbearing (see Tannen, 1994, 1998, for research on gender differences in communication). Evidence suggests that African American women faculty and administrators face the dual burdens of sexism and racism and also confront special challenges during the promotion and tenure process (Johnsrud and DesJarlais, 1994; O'Callaghan, 2007; Sandler, 1986; Singh, Robinson, and Williams-Greene, 1995). For example, organizational researchers have conclusively documented instances where race negatively influenced performance evaluations and ratings of promotion potential (Greenhaus and Parasuraman, 1993; Greenhaus, Parasuraman, and Wormley, 1990; Kraiger and Ford, 1985).

Conclusion

In summary, the barriers facing administrators of color, particularly females, are numerous. They include the large social realities of sexism and racism, which find expression in institutions of higher education in a multitude of ways. Often informed by these larger social barriers are the policies and practices of institutions of higher education that create and perpetuate barriers for people of color in specific educational organizations. The third category of barrier, internal barriers, is arguably the most contentious. Although we must be wary of blaming the victims, the research literature has identified specific barriers directly linked to internal psychological processes. Women of color face a distinct set of barriers that are linked to both race and gender, which may mean they have an exceptionally difficult time achieving professional success. As the following chapter illuminates, however, the research literature has also demonstrated some concrete strategies that administrators of color, especially females, may find useful in overcoming barriers to career advancement.

This chapter should serve as a clarion call for those institutions that have successfully removed barriers to career entry and advancement for administrators of color. Our request to those institutions is simple: find a venue and share your success stories. We can all learn from those who have succeeded where others continue to fail. We assert that it is time to shift the literature from documenting the frustrations, failures, challenges, and barriers to researching, highlighting, and replicating strategies for success.

Factors Influencing Engagement, Retention, and Advancement for Administrators of Color

T HE ENGAGEMENT, RETENTION, AND ADVANCEMENT of administrators of color have received increased attention in higher education over the past fifteen years (L. Benjamin, 1997; Jackson, 2001, 2004b, 2008; Mitchell, 1993; Rusher, 1996). This matter is of great importance as the literature begins to shift from an emphasis on identifying and describing the barriers facing administrators of color toward strategies that may be used to eliminate these barriers, thus cultivating a more diverse workforce in higher education. The previous chapter identified and discussed the barriers facing administrators of color, including social barriers, organizational and institutional barriers, and internal barriers, as well as the double burden of racism and sexism for women of color. This chapter discusses a model of engagement, retention, and advancement for administrators of color in higher education.

This chapter is organized into five sections: (1) understanding and borrowing from the successes in corporate management; (2) the necessity of mentoring and the integral role of leadership programs specifically for administrators of color; (3) strategies that educational institutions can use; (4) personal advancement strategies; and (5) a presentation of the engagement, retention, and advancement (ERA) model for administrators of color. The intent of this discussion is to provide concrete advice, recommendations, and strategies that can be used immediately in institutions of higher education.

Employment Challenges

Before beginning a discussion of retention and advancement, we must review the primary challenge to engaging and recruiting talented, qualified, and successful administrators of color for positions of leadership. This discussion is distinct from that of barriers in the previous chapter. Rather than focusing on what may stand in the way of professional success—success that would be achieved were it not for the barriers—the chief challenge to the recruitment of administrators of color is arguably the low numbers of people of color currently working in higher education. This situation is often referred to as the *pipeline problem*. This metaphor refers to the small number of African American tenured professors (Crase and Walker, 1988) and the even smaller numbers of individuals who have been matriculating through doctoral programs in recent years (Crase 1994; Crase and Hamrick, 1992; Reis and Thurgood, 1993). Additionally, although African American women outnumber African American males in higher education administration, the historical perception that women of color are "tokens" (Mosley, 1980) may persist. Additional lingering concerns for female administrators of color may include the belief that their positions are peripheral to the core work of the institution and the feelings of being overworked, underpaid, alienated, isolated, and unsupported in their work (Mosley, 1980).

Evidence suggests, however, that advancement opportunities exist for people of color in higher education and that increasing numbers are finding employment in higher education institutions (Fontaine and Greenlee, 1993; U.S. Department of Education, 2002). For example, with regard to opportunities for promotion in higher education, African American women were evenly split when asked whether they experienced greater difficulty advancing in the educational hierarchy than majority group members (Fontaine and Greenlee, 1993). Many African American women did not report feelings of frustration in their efforts to advance because of race or gender; however, they agreed unanimously that men advance faster than women in administration (Fontaine and Greenlee, 1993).

The same appears to hold true for opportunities to publish scholarly work, a recognized route to promotion. For example, Mosley (1980) noted that African Americans had not been provided with the same publishing opportunities as Whites, which was attributable in part to racist policies that denied African Americans access to the publishing medium. Additionally, as noted earlier, as recently as 1998 African American academic leaders had on average fewer than half as many career publications as White academic leaders (see Table 11). According to Simpson (2000), however, African American female administrators reported they were learned, well-read scholars who published in mainstream journals in their areas of expertise (Simpson, 2000).

Other studies (Esquibel, 1992; Gorena, 1996) have identified factors and forces that influence appointments to positions of leadership in higher education for Chicanos or Chicanas and Hispanics. In a qualitative study of sixty-eight Hispanic women who held senior administrative positions, Gorena (1996) identified five major factors respondents indicated as positively influencing advancement: (1) education and training, (2) goal setting, (3) networking, (4) knowledge of the mainstream system, and (5) knowledge of the advancement process. Earlier, Esquibel (1992) identified seven situational factors that influence the appointment of Chicano or Chicana administrators to senior-level positions of leadership: new initiatives (programs, workshops, incentive programs, lawsuits, and networking); contacts and political involvement; affirmative action plans and requirements; the emphasis an administrator puts on maintaining his or her roots; the ethnic composition of the institution and the community (also referred to as "the Chicano concentration"); contacts in the Chicano community; and personal advocates on governing boards, on screening committees, and in search firms.

Each of these factors provides us with an entry point into a new conversation, one focused on the recruitment, engagement, retention, and advancement for administrators of color into positions of leadership in higher education. The remainder of this chapter focuses on successful strategies and recommendations for how the higher education community can collectively eliminate the challenges to advancement for people of color and reduce the enduring effects of racism and sexism still present in academia.

Success in Corporate America: Lessons for Higher Education

As noted earlier, executives and employees of color in corporate and business America experience barriers to advancement (America and Anderson, 1996; Kern-Foxworth, 2000; McRae and Carter, 1992; Thomas and Gabarro, 1999), but the literature has grown that details success strategies for people of color in management. In *Breaking Through,* Thomas and Gabarro (1999) articulate the processes of development and advancement that produce minority executives. Based on the experiences of fifty-four executives and managers of color from three companies, Thomas and Gabarro examined both the individual and organizational factors that influence minority advancement. Although they assert that not much is known about the experiences of minorities who do break the race-based glass ceiling, they provide readers with concrete findings on how some corporations have created efforts to maintain diversity. First, senior management and key executives were committed to including people of color in the organization. Second, relationships were formed around the concept of equal opportunity, often bringing together White senior executives and change-oriented employees. Third, people of color were active participants in promoting change in the organization. Fourth, companies not only hired and retained employees of color but also successfully integrated them into the core functions of the business. Fifth, companies retained a focus on diversifying the very top levels of their organizational management teams. Last, racial diversity became an integral part of the company's identity, as evidenced by an alignment between their hiring and promotion policies and practices and institutional culture.

Thomas and Gabarro (1999) provided additional insights that may prove to be helpful. In reference to the education, social class, and family background of the sample, the study showed that the White executives and executives of color were from "structurally equivalent backgrounds" (p. 93), suggesting that members from each group entered the ranks of corporate management equally prepared to succeed. The study also revealed that executives of color were able to expand on their preprofessional experiences despite facing obstacles such as racism and discrimination. In essence, individuals who loved their work, were regarded highly by their peers, and were able to develop deep and meaningful relationships and specialized skills were the most likely to succeed.

A theme that has emerged in research on African Americans in management is the centrality of race to the experiences of African Americans in the workplace (Livers and Caver, 2003; Tucker, 1980). Rather than trying to suppress racial identity, many studies (Livers and Caver, 2003; Tucker, 1980) have revealed that African American managers often think of the way race affects their daily experiences and workplace accomplishments. As Tucker (1980) noted, the crux of the matter is to think through what it means to be an African American in a position of influence and power. For example, Livers and Caver (2003) note that often high expectations and standards for African American managers and employees can be motivating but also onerous. That is, African Americans are often given the responsibility of both setting and maintaining a diversity agenda in organizations.

In their 2001 book, *Our Separate Ways: Black and White Women and the Struggle for Professional Identity,* Bell and Nkomo describe African American female managers' efforts at changing perceived racial and gender bias in the workplace. Through targeted life-history interviews with eighty African American women and forty White women supplemented by in-depth, nationwide survey results from 725 African American and White managers, Bell and Nkomo compiled information on how women are able to overcome barriers in the workplace. Although very few women identified company policies or practices that assisted them, many were able to identify specific individuals who had been instrumental in their success. Perseverance, determination, and career mobility were also identified as factors contributing to advancement.

Kern-Foxworth (2000) explored the status of women of color in the workplace, identified cultural traditions and their connection to workplace performance, provided suggestions for helping women of color reach upper-level management positions in corporate America, and suggested strategies to help managers integrate women of color into the workplace. Specifically, Kern-Foxworth cites research suggesting that African American women experience oppression, exclusion from mainstream society, feelings of being different, low self-esteem, being barred from seeking better professional and personal opportunities, and a lack of equal opportunity (Dickens and Dickens, 1991). As a way to combat these feelings, Dickens and Dickens uncovered many characteristics of top-level African American managers, including having dreams and developing a vision, committing to it, and articulating this dream to others. Additional characteristics include setting high standards; displaying high energy, focus, dedication, purpose, and integrity; performing well under stress; motivating and rewarding people; developing a success style; taking ownership for their organization;

and taking charge of one's own professional and personal development (Dickens and Dickens, 1991).

In summary, the literature from business and organizational management provides leaders, most specifically African American leaders, in higher education a host of lessons, a "how-to" on how to provide support and encourage success for administrators of color. Many of these lessons stem from advice that pertains to individual perceptions and beliefs in one's own efficacy (Bell and Nkomo, 2001; Dickens and Dickens, 1991). Others, however, such as the lessons outlined by Thomas and Gabarro (1999) provide a road map for institutions interested in diversifying their workforce. One area often overlooked in the literature is the role of leadership programs in preparing administrators of color to make career advancements. The next section discusses this area of research in depth.

Role of Leadership Programs

In 1981, Frank called for more leadership programs designed specifically to prepare African American administrators. In making the case that the 1980s style of administrative diversity erred more toward tokenism, Frank stated, "If administrators—White administrators—are really serious about the needs of Black administrators in your predominantly White institutions, there is a need for more training programs designed to prepare Black administrators" (p. 22). Lindsay (1994) also called explicitly for "continuing professional education and development programs for gender and racial minorities" (p. 440) to assist African American females in moving toward leadership roles in faculty and administration. Not only researchers and practitioners request more opportunities to engage administrators of color in leadership programs; however. In particular, Mulnix, Bowden, and Lopez (2002) documented that leaders of educational institutions (in the case discussed, presidents of Hispanic-serving institutions) also strongly believe in the importance of institutional advancement opportunities and activities for people of color.

A modicum of research indexes and details the role of professional associations and leadership programs in promoting advancement opportunities for administrators of color (McCurtis, Jackson, and O'Callaghan, 2009).

For example, Lynch and Charleston (1990) provide a rich description of university training programs for American Indians that began in the 1970s located at Harvard University, the University of Minnesota, Pennsylvania State University, and Arizona State University. Additionally, at least two case studies in the research literature discuss an African American administrative leadership program at the University System of Georgia (Powell, 1991) and the Minority Administrators Program at the University of South Carolina (Thompson and Bjork, 1989).

To date, however, very little literature focuses specifically on leadership development for people of color in higher education (McCurtis, Jackson, and O'Callaghan, 2009). Much of the literature on leaders of color focuses on recruitment and retention (Jackson, 2001) but not on the actual preparation of leaders. Nevertheless, professional growth and development have been conceptualized as key components of retention and as benchmarks for campus diversity (Davis, 1994; Jackson, 2002; Jackson, 2004c). The research that has been identified tends to center predominantly on African Americans (women in particular), with little research on Hispanics, Latinos, and Latinas (Esquibel, 1992; Gorena, 1996; Haro, 1990; Martinez, 2005), Asian Americans (Fujimoto, 1996; Montez, 1998; Nakanishi, 1993), and American Indians (Kern-Foxworth, 2000; Lynch and Charleston, 1990; Swisher, 2001; Warner, 1995). A comprehensive analysis of leadership programs and initiatives in higher education for people of color has recently been developed (McCurtis, Jackson, and O'Callaghan, 2009; see also Leon, 2005). Moreover, although the literature has identified leadership programs as pivotal in the development of administrators of color, very little has been written about key components of the implementation of specific programs.

Results from the existing research demonstrate that most people of color who have successfully risen to leadership positions have participated in leadership development programs at some point during their careers (Cavanaugh, 2007; Holmes, 2004; Jenifer, 2005; McCurtis, Jackson, and O'Callaghan, 2009; Thomas, 2005). Yet leadership programs for people of color have primarily been reactive responses to the growing number of students of color on campuses (Harvey, 2005) to provide higher education with prepared and diverse leadership to address the increasingly complex political and social climate on campus (Thomas, 2005). One leadership preparation program, however, focused on the specific needs of minority-serving institutions. The Kellogg Minority Serving Institutions Leadership Fellows Program is a joint pilot effort supported by the W.K. Kellogg Foundation, the Alliance for Equity in Higher Education, the Hispanic Association of Colleges and Universities, the American Indian Higher Education Consortium, and the National Association for Equal Opportunity in Higher Education (McCurtis, Jackson, and O'Callaghan, 2009; Merisotis and Aveilhe, 2005). This program has the explicit purpose of preparing leaders to work at minority-serving institutions that have a distinct culture and face a set of challenges different from those present at predominantly White institutions (McCurtis, Jackson, and O'Callaghan, 2009). Two-year colleges have been the most successful thus far in implementing leadership programs and, compared with four-year institutions, appear to be particularly focused on developing leaders of color and women (Pierce, Mahoney, and Kee, 1996).

In addition to mapping the landscape of leadership development opportunities for people of color, scholars have recognized the importance of organizational and institutional support as it relates to creating and implementing such training. For example, among Esquibel's thirteen recommendations for institutions of higher education and six recommendations for higher education organizations (1992) are the development of specific institutes to train Chicanos and Chicanas for various areas of administration in higher education and workshops specifically for aspiring Chicano Chicana administrators. Although the research on the effectiveness and applicability of such leadership programs and initiatives has yet to be documented and disseminated on a large scale, the call for a continued commitment to leadership programs for aspiring administrators and leaders of color remains loud and clear.

The Importance of Mentoring

In *Rites of Passage and Rights of Way,* Phyllis Green (1997) describes her experiences as an African American female administrator with a fifteen-year career at three different public universities. Knowingly or not, Green's writing serves as a road map for aspiring female administrators and African American females in particular. Green's chapter does not deal directly with the importance of mentoring, but it provides critical information, the kind often shared between mentors and protégés: a discussion of institutional culture, power, and change, and how young women may navigate their ways through these powerful but often hidden forces. Additionally, stemming from research on sixty-eight Hispanic women holding senior administrative positions in institutions of higher education nationwide, Gorena (1996) noted that knowledge of the institutional process for advancement and mentoring were keys to their career successes.

As part of a greater discussion in the career success of African Americans, Cokley, Dreher, and Stockdale (2004) document both the importance of mentoring for African Americans and the differential access African Americans have to same-race mentors because of the dearth of African American leaders in many organizations. Yet at the same time these researchers and others note that having a mentor is critical to a successful career (Cokley, Dreher, and Stockdale, 2004; Dreher and Ash, 1990; Dreher and Cox, 1996). In a 1993 study, Fontaine and Greenlee sampled twelve African American female faculty and administrators from colleges and universities in the commonwealth of Virginia. The study revealed multiple factors that could mediate barriers to career advancement. One of the major factors contributing to the success of Black women was having a good mentor (Fontaine and Greenlee, 1993). In a broad discussion of the importance of mentoring, Johnson (1997) outlines three types of mentoring available to women in higher education.

Informal mentoring is a relationship that does not have any of the markers of a formal mentor-protégé arrangement. For example, the mentoring relationship has no specific meeting times or explicit expectations. The content of an informal mentoring relationship varies but may include simple advisory conversations about research and career options or may extend to more personal issues such as how to navigate an organization's politics. In contrast, *formal mentoring* uses a structured time frame and often sets out performance expectations for both the mentor and protégé. One important aspect of these arrangements is that they are often institutionalized and supported by educational or professional organizations. Some of the topics covered include effective networking, how to balance work and family life, and issues related to community service.

Peer mentoring occurs on a professional level between and "among people at a similar level of authority and decision making" (Johnson, 1998, p. 54).

Mentoring, Johnson notes, provides an important means of increasing both the number of African American women serving as administrators in higher education and the percentage of those who reach senior-level positions. Additionally, she provides readers and scholars with an inversion of the "double discrimination" dilemma faced by many African American women by suggesting that African American women administrators can be effective mentors precisely because they bring to their jobs distinctive and diverse perspectives as both women and minorities.

In reporting research on White and African American female deans from Research I and II institutions, Lindsay (1994) noted that mentors are the single most important factor in the career development of administrators. The respondents in Lindsay's research (1994) described mentors as being "instrumental" in "remov[ing] obstacles to . . . advancement and productivity" and "very supportive" in encouraging research, including coauthoring papers and providing introductions and recommendations for career advancement (pp. 435–436). In a subsequent publication, Lindsay (1999) again revealed the importance of mentoring to the career success of African American women. Through semistructured interviews with three African American female presidents and one provost, Lindsay established that support groups are key in building professional support networks and providing a forum for discussions about "tactic building" among African American female administrative leaders.

In attempting to discern the characteristics and activities leading to career advancement and achievement for African American administrators, Bridges (1996) identified mentoring relationships as playing an integral role. Of the participant group, more than 95 percent rated the importance of a mentoring relationship to their achievement as "important," "very important," or "crucial." Bridges asserted that African American administrators, to promote success, should identify professors or teachers who can serve as mentors and recognize the importance of professional support by serving as a mentor to others.

In 2003, Jackson and Flowers published an article on retaining African American student affairs professionals. The study used the Delphi method to create a panel of experts. The six administrators (four male, two female; three vice presidents for student affairs, two deans of students, and one associate vice president for student affairs) all worked at predominantly White institutions.

From their findings, Jackson and Flowers outline specific strategies to improve the retention of African American student affairs administrators, which include developing or supporting opportunities for mentoring.

What Universities Can Do

Although two specific initiatives (leadership and mentoring programs) have been linked with an increase in the recruitment, retention, and advancement of administrators of color (see Bridges, 1996; Jackson and Flowers, 2003; Lindsay, 1999), institutions, in an effort to increase diversity of the workforce, have a responsibility to engage, implement, and sustain these activities. Some suggestions for activities that institutions should consider supporting are listed in the following paragraph (McCurtis, Jackson, and O'Callaghan, 2009).

Mentoring and Support Groups

Institutions should do all they can to provide support for mentoring programs for aspiring leaders of color (Jackson, 2001). For example, Abney and Richey (1991) note that institutions should start support groups, initiate mentoring programs, and help interested African American women grow professionally in their fields. As part of a comprehensive retention strategy, Jackson and Flowers (2003) also suggest that institutions develop or support mentoring opportunities to keep African American student affairs administrators at predominantly White institutions.

A Multicultural and Diverse Campus Environment

The successful recruitment of African American scholars and administrative leaders has been linked with having a healthy multicultural environment on campus (Crase, 1994). Recommendations for the successful recruitment of administrators of color include the presence of campus- and systemwide campaigns designed to highlight the benefits of diversity (Lindsay, 1999). Recruitment of African American administrators has even been suggested as an appropriate benchmark for establishing a campus's receptivity to diversity (Davis, 1994; Jackson, 2001). As it relates specifically to African American women, Williams (1989) recommends that those considering careers at predominantly

White institutions ensure that the college president and chancellor see hiring and promoting people of color as an administrative priority. Williams also recommends making sure the academic community is receptive to African Americans and women in policy-making positions. Relying on interviews with three African American women and three White women who were or are deans or associate deans, Lindsay (1997) recommends policy for ensuring the presence of African American female deans and associate deans. Chief among them is the institution's clear recognition that a racial problem (underrepresentation) exists.

According to Sanders and Mellow (1990, p. 9), "Throughout the last two decades, higher education has struggled to incorporate diversity into its curriculum, its student body, and its professional staff. Yet as colleges and universities turn their heads toward the twenty-first century, the landscape in front of them is all too familiar—still too White, too male, too Eurocentric. . . . The power of tradition and past practice in higher education militate against the diversity it so desperately needs." Although these remarks may still ring true, research clearly indicates that being receptive to diversity and multiculturalism on college campuses will likely increase the numbers of administrators and leaders of color working in higher education. Although the section presented here is brief in an attempt to cover the range of ways that universities and colleges can increase the presence of administrators of color, the role of an open campus environment receptive to diversity in all its forms should not be underestimated.

Affirmative Action

The recruitment of administrative leaders of color has been greater in institutions that adhere to the principles of affirmative action, both in spirit and law (Lindsay, 1997). In turn, African American professionals have indicated they perceive affirmative action programs and policies to be effective ways to remedy past discriminatory practices (Brown and Globetti, 1991). For example, Jackson (2001) describes retention strategies for predominantly White institutions interested in retaining African American administrators. The results from Jackson's study indicate institutions must commit to the principles of diversity and affirmative action and provide equity in wages and salaries to support the professional advancement and development of administrators of color. Additionally, Jackson and Flowers in a 2003 study noted that institutions must communicate and integrate a philosophy of fairness into the campus environment to be successful in retaining African American administrators.

Balance Between Work and Life

Ensuring flexibility in positions of leadership and power is another key retention strategy for institutions interested in retaining female administrators of color. For example, Twombly (1998) suggests flexibility should be available for women with full-time appointments to work part-time when necessary, and time limits should not be applied to potential promotions. This area of scholarship is relatively new, and most research is centered on female faculty. Research, practice, and information on the benefits to individuals and institutions as a result of ensuring flexible working conditions are still forthcoming. For example, Mason and Goulden (2002, 2004a, 2004b) have been conducting research using results from the University of California Faculty Work and Family Survey and Survey of Doctorate Recipients. Thus far, their results have demonstrated that female faculty with children are more likely than male faculty to experience stressful parenting and greater conflicts in balancing their professional demands with their parenting obligations (Mason and Goulden, 2004b; see also Ward and Wolf-Wendel, 2004).

Other research conducted by Mason and Goulden (2002) suggests that child rearing is time intensive and that structural changes to employment programs sensitive to this fact will be successful in attempting to retain highly qualified female academics. They suggest modified leave, active service policies, and revisions to the current tenure process (stopping the tenure clock when a family has children) and benefits packages that include family leave policies and flexible scheduling opportunities. Other recommendations for retaining female faculty include early career counseling, mentoring programs, and accommodations for dual-career couples. The most revolutionary suggestions put forth by Mason and Goulden (2002) include a redefinition of what it means to be a ladder-rank, tenure-track faculty member: instituting part-time programs, codifying reentry policies, and accepting the fact some faculty will not be able to be as productive in some years.

Fairness in Recruitment, Hiring, and Promotion

The appearance and codification of fairness in the employment process can go far in recruiting and retaining administrators and leaders of color. Crase (1994) notes that recruitment strategies must include a strong commitment to diversity, including identifying and employing minority individuals. One strategy to accomplish these goals is to use qualified administrators whose academic credentials are in a field that complements higher and postsecondary education (business administration). Another is to identify minority doctoral students or existing faculty of color who show administrative potential and provide them with leadership opportunities and experiences. Lindsay (1999) adds that institutions should be certain to include people of color on search committees, and Williams (1989) asserts that institutions must develop strategic plans for advancement training for all employees, including employees of color. To be successful in retaining people of color in leadership positions, organizational leaders must encourage the identification and vocational nurturing of those who demonstrate potential for leadership. And salaries for leaders of color in higher education administration should be both attractive to potential candidates (who may have other offers from private industry or corporate management) and representative or reflective of actual job responsibilities and contributions to the institution (Jackson and Flowers, 2003; Williams, 1989).

What Individual Administrators Can Do

Research studies have identified specific steps and strategies for individuals to pursue to ensure a successful career. For example, researchers have noted that to improve career opportunities, administrators of color must be confident (Abney and Richey, 1991; Bridges, 1996), develop and maintain a positive sense of self (Abney and Richey, 1991), be inspired to meet challenges (Abney and Richey, 1991), be qualified and competent for leadership roles (Abney and Richey, 1991), and be actively involved in professional associations and organizations (Abney and Richey, 1991; Gorena, 1996). Additional items include having strong written and oral communication skills (Bridges, 1996; Fontaine and Greenlee, 1993; Rolle, Davies, and Banning, 2000), having strong personal and family support systems (Fontaine and Greenlee, 1993; Gorena, 1996; Wolfman, 1997), being a workaholic (Fontaine and Greenlee, 1993; Miller, 1991), and being highly motivated to succeed (Fontaine and Greenlee, 1993). Bridges's research (1996) suggests that many of these qualities can be attained by educational preparation and achievement, especially in the form of a terminal degree (Esquibel, 1992; Gorena, 1996; Miller, 1991; Rolle, Davies, and Banning, 2000).

Miller (1991) advises that administrators of color prepare in advance for rejection because, when individuals experience career failure or frustration, they should prepare to take a new approach or direction and persevere through the difficult time. One suggested strategy for managing these processes is to seek out friends and colleagues to talk about the challenges. These sounding boards may be individuals who have experienced similar frustrations or mentors who are able to provide sound advice on how to navigate difficult times.

As noted, African American women and other women of color may alleviate tensions and adjust to the dual barriers of race and gender through family, church, and community connections (Gorena, 1996; Wolfman, 1997). For example, many African American female administrators indicated their children and husbands contributed to their emotional stability by assisting in household responsibilities. As relayed by Wolfman (1997), church was described as a place where women have long found meaningful relationships and opportunities for leadership roles through prayer circles, avocational clubs, Sunday schools, fundraising activities, and other social events. The church was described as serving as "the center of the black family life" (Wolfman, 1997, p. 165). Although some women were adamant about separating their personal and professional lives, Wolfman (1997) notes that in the African American tradition, "social units are buffers against a hostile world and a means of maintaining a sense of equilibrium" (p. 166). Gorena's research (1996) also indicated that having the support of family was key in securing professional success for Hispanic women.

Three additional themes emerge from Rolle, Davies, and Banning's interviews with senior-level academic administrators (2000). Their advice to the budding African American administrative professional includes self-assurance, boldness, and assertiveness as "key ingredient[s] needed by black people who desire to enter higher education administration" (p. 90). They also identified good communications skills (both written and oral) and a robust understanding of the relationship between politics and education in society as critical to career success (see also Gorena, 1996).

An Emerging Model

One way to synthesize the information presented in this chapter is to consider it part of a model of engagement, retention, and advancement for administrators of color. In 2004, Jackson presented an emerging engagement, retention, and advancement model for African American administrators at predominantly White institutions in an edited book written by and for African American faculty and graduate students in higher education (2004a).

As Jackson noted, the model of engagement, retention, and advancement is captured in four parts: (1) preengagement, (2) engagement, (3) advancement, and (4) outcomes (Figure 6). Underlying the model is the prescriptive assumption that interested institutions are actively engaged in relationships with the surrounding African American community and that these same institutions are firmly committed to the principles of diversity and affirmative action. Phase I of the model (preengagement) describes the process by which the institution begins its relationship with a future recruit. This phase essentially sets the stage for all future interactions. It actually begins before the candidate's arrival on campus and before any formalized interaction has occurred. Two additional components make up Phase I: (1) a formal orientation program that introduces the candidate to the school and community, and (2) a competitive, equitable incentive package.

The second phase of the model, engagement, begins when the candidate accepts official duties and essentially becomes engaged with the campus community and begins to understand his or her assigned roles, responsibilities, rights, and privileges. This phase is characterized by multiple components, including empowerment, access to leadership opportunities, access to mentoring, and in-service professional development, which supplement administrators' skills with context-specific information. Advancement, the third phase, may be the most important consideration in retention. This phase may encompass

FIGURE 6

The Engagement, Retention, and Advancement Model for African Americans in the Higher Education Administrative Workforce

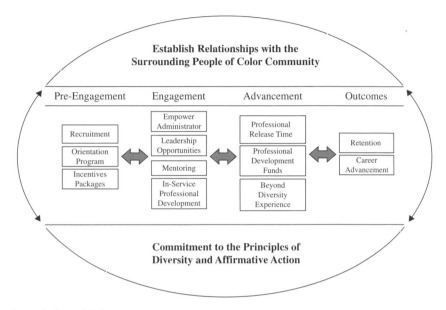

Source: Jackson, 2004a.

measures for professional release time (to pursue professional development and to compensate for the "unpaid" hours advising), funds to pursue these professional activities, and opportunities "beyond the diversity mission of the institution" (Jackson, 2004a, p. 218).

The final phase, outcomes, is assessed in two parts: the actual retention of administrators and measurable career advancement. Essentially, retention of African American administrators and their career advancement is measured in relation to White administrators. The underlying supposition of the model is that the more positive the links among preengagement, engagement, retention, and advancement, the more likely an African American administrator (or other administrators of color) will be to remain in an administrative position. As noted by Jackson (2004a), the presentation of this model, one of the first such models introduced into the higher education literature, is only the beginning in a long process of empirical testing and refinement. Although the model was built on the findings of studies of African American administrators at predominantly White institutions, the model could be extended and tested against the experiences of other administrators of color at both predominantly White institutions and other institutional types.

Conclusion

This chapter has laid the groundwork necessary to reduce and remove various types of barriers to the career advancement of administrators of color. The engagement, retention, and advancement model provides the structure in which individuals and organizations can implement many of the critical strategies for success in one's career, affirmed in the research literature laid out in this chapter. The suggestions provided include ways in which institutions and professional associations can assist in diversification efforts as well as many items that administrators of color can be attentive to in their own lives to ensure they are giving themselves every opportunity for advancement. These measures provide concrete strategies to be used to combat racism and sexism and to aid in eliminating them from our institutions of higher education.

Concluding Remarks Regarding the Importance of a Racially Diverse Administrative Workforce

T HE PREVIOUS CHAPTERS REVIEWED published literature detailing critical information about the work life realities and experiences of administrators of color. Original data analysis was integrated in the second chapter to provide a national context against which to juxtapose the published literature. Although they are not typically included in these monographs, original data were necessary in this case to fill a glaring omission in the knowledge base. The inclusion of these data permits us to provide a balanced perspective regarding the current challenges and opportunities for and presence of administrators of color in the higher education administrative workforce.

A chief purpose of this monograph is to help clarify the literature on administrators of color. Although scholars have been examining the topic for at least three decades, in general this body of work is sparse and eclectic. That is, the general sense is that knowledge about administrators of color in higher education is lacking. It is unclear why the topic has been largely ignored in the literature, especially compared with other related key topics such as students of color in higher education. One explanation could be that people of color were historically not part of the leadership landscape; thus, little formal analysis and categorization of the work were conducted.

At this juncture, however, we are fortunate enough to have a critical mass of publications on the topic of administrators of color to form a body of knowledge. This chapter organizes and synthesizes those studies to bring the knowledge base from the peripheral of the field to core knowledge. First, it discusses the emergent and aggregate challenges for administrators of color in higher education, focusing on the challenges presented by the data on administrators of color detailed in the second chapter. Second, it builds on these challenges to highlight critical areas needing future research. Last, it provides practice-based suggestions on how to respond to these challenges.

Emergent and Aggregate Challenges for Administrators of Color

The next session highlights challenges that emerged from the synthesis of the literature. The synthesis focused on macro-level themes across the literature on administrators of color. Likewise, this section highlights aggregate challenges that are derived from original data analysis of the national databases used in the development of this monograph.

Emergent Challenges

This subsection provides a concise synthesis of the challenges for administrators of color that emerged from the literature. Present work conditions for people of color in higher education are viewed as a byproduct of past segregation in the United States (Bielby and Baron, 1984; Lee, 1997; Lindsay, 1999), which has created both race and gender segregation in employment patterns in higher education (Davison and Burke, 2000; Jackson, 2008). For example, race and sex segregation exist in nonteaching positions in higher education: Whites are more likely to be faculty or administrative executives, and Blacks or Hispanics are more likely to be clerical workers (Lee, 1997). Likewise, women dominate the clerical, administrative, other professional, technical, and paraprofessional occupations. Unfortunately, employment trends seem to support continued segregation in the professoriat, with women and people of color concentrated in lower levels (assistant professor and non-tenure-track positions) (Lindsay, 1999).

The inclusion of administrators and faculty of color on college campuses grew out of the student protests of the 1960s (Jones, 1997; Mosley, 1980; Smith, 1980). These riots compelled universities to hire African Americans in key roles to help respond to the racially based unrest. Smith (1980) notes that many of these appointments were made to appease the African American community and to maintain the flow of federal dollars to the institutions.

Although they were positions of authority, they unfortunately lacked power in the formal administrative structure commensurate with that authority.

The concept of affirmative action is not universally accepted as a positive employment practice or philosophy (Brown and Globetti, 1991; Mosley, 1980). It was found that people of color and White women were more likely to be hired in positions previously held by people of color (Konrad and Pfeffer, 1991) and that administrators of color were most likely to work in less prestigious organizations and in lower-level positions (Chenoweth, 1998; Konrad and Pfeffer, 1991). The high-level positions that administrators of color historically held were well respected but often had little authority or control over institutional change (Frank, 1981; Smith, 1980). For example, African American administrators were given responsibility for affirmative action programming and for African American or ethnic studies or student services (Frank, 1981). These positions were often viewed as dead-end jobs, often funded by soft money with no real commitment from the institution. Most often, they were staff rather than line positions, with few opportunities for transition or advancement (Frank, 1981).

Administrators of color often perform expanded roles (role modeling, mentoring, and community relations) in addition to formal institutional responsibilities (Jackson, 2001; Tucker, 1980). In describing the expectations of African American administrators, Tucker (1980) noted that faculty members and administrators were expected to be a combination of politician, social director, ombudsman, and problem solver. In a contemporary context, Martinez (1999) noted that many Latino and Hispanic administrators emphasized social justice issues in their work (such as access for low-income students) at the risk of being singled out for being too radical or too advocacy minded.

Mentoring is a key function in supporting and promoting administrators of color and women. Previous research (see Crase, 1994; Fontaine and Greenlee, 1993; Gorena, 1996; Jackson, 2003b; Johnson, 1998; Lindsay, 1994) found that mentors, support groups, and networking are important professional development activities for administrators of color in higher education. These activities and support initiatives improve work conditions and outcomes as well as the chance for success for administrators of color in higher education. Fontaine and Greenlee (1993) found that a major factor contributing to the success of Black women was good mentors; Gorena (1996) found similar results for Hispanic women.

Race plays a vital role in every aspect of their administrative careers for people of color in higher education. In a study of African American administrators at predominantly White institutions, Rolle, Davies, and Banning (2000) found that race played a role in virtually every aspect of their administrative careers. Consequently, people of color have felt pressure to behave professionally like White males. In tracking the employment trends, progress, and barriers for women of color in academic administration, Wilson (1989) noted the tremendous pressure that women of color reported in feeling as though they need to behave like White males to be successful in their positions.

Women of color experience a double jeopardy in higher education, one of the most highly cited obstacles for them (Gorena, 1996; Howard-Hamilton and Williams, 1996; Lindsay, 1994; Singh, Robinson, and Williams-Greene, 1995; Wilson, 1989). The terms "double jeopardy," "dual burden," "double bind," and "interactive discrimination" have been used interchangeably to connote a set of conflicting expectations and pressures that may be created when an individual is considered to have membership in two distinct minority groups. These similar struggles were found for women across all racial and ethnic groups (Gorena, 1996). In contrast to the work on women of color, few studies focused on males of color in administration (Jackson, 2001, 2006a).

Aggregated Challenges

This section discusses data (modes and means) to highlight aggregate challenges for administrators of color based on information from the second chapter. The discussion is arranged according to employment section: academic leaders and student affairs administrators. The academic workforce in higher education is mostly male (Exhibit 2). The mode for all racial or ethnic categories was male, except for blacks/African Americans (52.8 percent female). The reverse is true for student affairs administrators (Exhibit 3). That is, student affairs professionals are mostly female, except for Whites.

The mode rank for Whites and Asian American/Pacific Islanders was full professor, while for Blacks/African Americans it was associate professor and for Hispanics was "other," highlighting challenges previously detailed for

EXHIBIT 2
Mode and Mean Data on the Academic Workforce by Race or Ethnicity

Factors	Race/Ethnicity			
	Black/African American	Hispanic	White, Non-Hispanic	Asian American/ Pacific Islander
Gender	Female	Male	Male	Male
Level of Education	Doctorate	Master's	Doctorate	Doctorate/Master's
Age	45–55	45–55	45–55	45–55
Principal Activity	Teaching	Teaching	Teaching	Teaching
Professorial Rank	Associate	Other	Full	Full
Total Earned Income	$60,699	$55,089	$72,883	$75,319
Primary Disciplinary Field	Education/Caring	Education/Caring	All Other	All Other/Caring
Institutional Type	Research/ Comprehensive/ Liberal Arts	Comprehensive	Research	Research
Institutional Control	Public 4-Year	Public 4-Year	Public 4-Year	Public 4-Year
Region	Southeast	Southeast	Southeast	Far West
Career Publications	10.4	20.8	25.1	35.1
Career Presentations	49.4	58.3	63.2	80.6

Note: American Indians/Alaska Natives were excluded from the exhibit because most sample sizes were too small.
Source: National Study of Postsecondary Faculty: 1999.

EXHIBIT 3
Mode and Mean Data for Student Affairs Administrators by Race or Ethnicity

Factors	Race/Ethnicity				
	Black/African American	Hispanic	White, Non-Hispanic	Asian American/Pacific Islander	
Gender	Female	Female	Male	Female	
Level of Education	Master's	Master's	Master's	Master's	
Institutional Size (Student Enrollment)	10,000–19,999	10,000–19,999	1,000–2,499	2,500–4,999	
Total Earned Income	$84,587	$77,643	$71,614	$90,262	
Institution Type	University	University	University	University	
Institutional Control	Public	Public	Public	Public	
Region	III (Southeast)	III (Southeast)	III (Southeast)	VI (Southwest)	

Note: American Indians/Alaska Natives were excluded from the exhibit because most sample sizes were too small.
Source: National Association of Student Personnel Administrators Salary Survey, 1999.

Blacks/African Americans and Hispanics regarding securing senior-level positions in higher education. Mean income data show that Whites and Asian Americans/Pacific Islanders make as much as $20,000 more than Blacks/African Americans and Hispanics. In student affairs, the salary distribution is different. Although Asian Americans/Pacific Islanders are the highest paid, Blacks/African Americans are next, followed by Hispanics and then Whites. Blacks/African Americans produced the smallest number of career publications and career presentations, followed by Hispanics, Whites, and Asians/Pacific Islanders (the greatest number).

Directions for Future Research

This monograph provides numerous signposts for future research on diversifying the administrative workforce in higher education. The following suggestions stem from findings in this monograph and extend the work of previous scholars. This section should serve as a call to researchers invested in ensuring ethnic and racial administrative diversity in higher education. First is the need for outcomes-based research on the efficacy of leadership and mentoring programs for administrators of color. Building on the work of McCurtis, Jackson, and O'Callaghan (2009), research that documents how these programs are designed and enacted is crucial. How does participation in these programs translate into advanced career opportunities for individual administrators of color? What professional development activities are highlighted in these programs and which are the most effective? What benefits do participants in these programs accrue?

Second, the efficacy of university-initiated programs, policies, and initiatives should be assessed. General efforts to diversify individual campuses should be reviewed and replicated. Specifically, it should be determined whether campuses are in alignment with affirmative action plans, where they are legal, and whether these plans have successfully increased diversity in the senior levels of university administration. In brief, they include support of leadership and mentoring programs; a multicultural and diverse campus environment; the principles of affirmative action in recruitment, hiring, and promotion; and programs to ensure a balance between work and life (see the previous chapter for more detailed information on specific initiatives and programs).

Third, efforts should be renewed to replicate and extend previous qualitative research that has assessed the personal experiences of administrators in higher education (Coleman, 1998; Crase, 1994; Green, 1997; Howard-Hamilton and Williams, 1996; Mosley 1980; Watson, 2001). Specifically, the experiences of administrators of color at predominantly White institutions and minority-serving institutions should be analyzed. Some interesting research questions include a consideration of the climate at each institution and how it is conducive to diversity (Jackson and Daniels, 2006). Has the climate changed over time and if so, how? Has it become more inclusive or more exclusive, and in what ways? What is the governance structure at each institution, and how are resources distributed to encourage diversity and the hiring of administrators of color? Last, building on Jackson's work (2004a), research is needed that tests the engagement, retention, and advancement model with employment data from the higher education workforce. As one of the most recently developed models of engagement, retention, and advancement for people of color in higher education administration, it is necessary that this model be tested to discern its effectiveness as an explanatory tool to inform administrative practice and institutional decision making.

Implications for Practice

Although the previous section notes multiple areas for future research, there is no need to wait for research results before implementing programs and policies on campus. Some suggestions for practitioners and key decision makers about where to place staff, time, and money to encourage efforts to diversify the top levels of administration follow.

Choose a framework to begin conversations on campus regarding racial and ethnic diversity initiatives, referring to the list in the third chapter to generate conversations among human resources personnel, legal counsel, and senior leaders on campus.

Following the blueprint presented in the second chapter, analyze institutional data to identify barriers for people of color at your institution. Work with institutional researchers to determine areas of administration that are not diversified. Target subsequent engagement, recruitment, and retention efforts at these particular divisions.

Using previous qualitative research findings as a starting point, conduct interviews to determine what works on your campus. Speak with members of your administration and determine their feelings about working with a diverse workforce. Use the findings to support your efforts to increase racial and ethnic diversity.

Replicate programs and practices with proven success. Initiate mentoring, leadership training, and professional development programs for administrators of color on your campus.

In consultation with legal counsel, establish and ensure fair hiring and promotion practices. Discern whether an affirmative action hiring plan is appropriate for your institution and, if so, implement one.

Review successes and persistent challenges at your institution regularly. Continually evaluate your efforts and identify programs and policies needing improvement and additional attention. As noted in the first chapter, it is through these efforts that your institution will be able to use diversity data on administrators as a benchmark for commitment to overall institutional diversity.

Celebrate and highlight improvements at your institution. Contact professional associations, trade journals, and media outlets to inform them of your success at recruiting, retaining, and promoting a diverse administrative workforce. Be sure to also inform your local community and campus.

Conclusion

This monograph provides policymakers, administrators, faculty, researchers, and governing board members with information about diversifying the administrative ranks of colleges and universities in terms of race or ethnicity. Each chapter takes a specific perspective on the issue and presents relevant information. The first chapter identifies racial and ethnic administrative diversity as an area needing scholarly research, the second a much-needed national portrait of administrators broken down by racial and ethnic characteristics, the third persistent barriers and challenges faced by administrators of color, and the fourth critical information useful to eliminating such barriers. The four research questions presented in the first chapter are answered, with many resources suggested that are available to individuals concerned about racial and ethnic diversity on campus. Although the problem of underrepresentation endures on campuses across the United States, let this monograph be a call for change in administrative practices to include a more diverse and inclusive workforce.

Notes

1. National Study of Postsecondary Faculty: 1999 (NSOPF:99), used complex sampling and applied appropriate weights to equal the total population of postsecondary faculty—956,616. The NASPA Salary Survey (1999) included a random sample of 419 institutions that were deemed representative of the member institutions of NASPA—3,510.
2. The authors acknowledge that more nuanced experiences exist in ethnic and racial groups (for example, Hmong) masked by the labels used in this chapter and elsewhere in this monograph. We use these broad categories in this monograph, however, because they align with the manner in which the national data used were collected.
3. The NASPA database did not contain variables aligned with Carnegie's institutional classification but did provide a modified classification system: two-year institutions, four-year colleges, and four-year universities.
4. The legal term "protected class" describes groups of individuals that share common characteristics and are accordingly protected from discrimination and harassment under the law. Depending on jurisdiction (state or federal), they include but are not limited to race, sex, age, and disability status.

References

Abney, R., and Richey, D. (1991). Barriers encountered by Black female athletic administrators and coaches. *Journal of Physical Education, Recreation & Dance, 62*(6), 19–21.

Allen, W. R. (1992). The color of success: Outcomes at predominantly White and historically African American public colleges and universities. *Harvard Educational Review, 62,* 26–44.

America, R. F., and Anderson, B. E. (1996). *Soul in management: How African-American managers thrive in the competitive corporate environment.* Secaucus, NJ: Carol Publishing Group.

Barr, M. J. (1990). Growing staff diversity and changing career paths. In M. J. Barr, M. C. Upcraft, and Associates (Eds.), *New futures for student affairs: Building a vision for professional leadership and practice,* pp. 160–177. San Francisco: Jossey-Bass.

Bell, E.L.J.E., and Nkomo, S. M. (2001). *Our separate ways: Black and white women and the struggle for professional identity.* Boston: Harvard Business School Press.

Benjamin, L. (Ed.). (1997). *Black women in the academy: Promises and perils.* Gainesville: University Press of Florida.

Benjamin, P. (1997). Women chief executives and their approaches towards equity at American universities. *Comparative Education, 35*(2), 187–199.

Bennefield, R. M. (1999). Trench warriors: On the front lines. *Black Issues in Higher Education, 16,* 69–71.

Berry, T. R., and Mizelle, N. D. (Eds.) (2006). *From oppression to grace: Women of color and their dilemmas in the academy.* Sterling, VA: Stylus Publishing.

Bielby, W. T., and Baron, J. N. (1984). A women's place is with other women: Sex segregation within organizations. In B. F. Reskin (Ed.), *Sex segregation in the workplace* (pp. 27–55). Washington, DC: National Academy.

Braddock, J. H., II, and McPartland, J. M. (1987). How minorities continue to be excluded from equal employment opportunities: Research on labor market and institutional barriers. *Journal of Social Issues, 43*(1), 5–39.

Bridges, C. R. (1996). The characteristics of career achievement perceived by African American college administrators. *Journal of Black Studies, 26*(6), 748–767.

Brown, C. L., and Globetti, E. C. (1991). Perceptions and experiences of African American student affairs professionals. *College Student Affairs Journal, 11,* 3–10.

Cabrera, A. F., and others. (1999). Campus racial climate and the adjustment of students to college: A comparison between white students and African American students. *Journal of Higher Education, 70*(2), 134–160.

Cavanaugh, C. (2007). *The ACE fellows program: The benefits and values to ACE fellows.* Pensacola, FL: American Council on Education.

Chenoweth, K. (1998). African American college presidents in decline. *Black Issues in Higher Education, 15*(6), 20–25.

Chliwniak, L. (1997). *Higher education leadership: Analyzing the gender gap.* ASHE-ERIC Higher Education Report (Vol. 25). Washington, DC: George Washington University.

Cohen, A. M. (1998). *The shaping of American higher education: Emergence and growth of the contemporary system.* San Francisco: Jossey-Bass.

Cokley, K., Dreher, G. F., and Stockdale, M. S. (2004). Toward the inclusiveness and career success of African Americans in the workplace. In M. S. Stockdale and F. J. Crosby (Eds.), *The psychology and management of workplace diversity* (pp. 168–190). Malden, MA: Blackwell Publishing.

Coleman, J. (1998). *Barriers to career advancement by African-American and Caucasian female administrators in Minnesota organizations: A perception or reality?* Paper presented at an annual meeting of the American Educational Research Association, April 13–17, San Diego, CA.

Cook, B., and Codova, D. I. (2006). *Minorities in higher education: Twenty-second annual status report.* Washington, DC: American Council on Education.

Cooper, H. M. (1982). Scientific guidelines for conducting integrative research reviews. *Review of Educational Research, 52,* 291–302.

Cotter, D. A., Hermsen, J. M., Ovadia, S., and Vanneman, R. (2001). The glass ceiling effect. *Social Forces, 80*(2), 655–681.

Crase, D. (1994). The minority connection: African Americans in administrative/leadership positions. *Physical Educator, 51*(1), 15–21.

Crase, D., and Hamrick, M. H. (1992). Distribution of minority doctorates in physical education. *Physical Educator, 49*(4), 174–179.

Crase, D., and Walker, H. (1988). The black physical educator: An endangered species. *Journal of Physical Education, Recreation & Dance, 59*(8), 65–69.

Crenshaw, K. (1991). Mapping the margins: Intersectionality, identity politics and violence against women of color. *Stanford Law Review, 43*(6), 1241–1279.

Davis, J. D. (1994). Queenie: A case study on racial, cultural and gender dimensions of leadership. In J. D. Davis (Ed.), *Coloring the halls of ivy: Leadership and diversity in the academy* (pp. 113–122). Bolton, MA: Anker Publishing Company.

Davison, K. H., and Burke, M. J. (2000). Sex discrimination in simulated selection contexts: A meta-analytic study. *Journal of Vocational Behavior, 56,* 225–248.

Dickens, F., Jr., and Dickens, J. (1991). *The black manager: Making it in the corporate world.* New York: AMACOM.

Dougherty, R. (1980). The black female administrator: Women in a double bind. In S. K. Biklen and M. B. Brannigan (Eds.), *Women in educational leadership* (pp.124–148). Lexington, MA: Lexington Books.

Dreher, G. F., and Ash, R. A. (1990). A comparative study of mentoring among men and women in managerial, professional, and technical positions. *Journal of Applied Psychology, 75*, 539–546.

Dreher, G. F., and Cox, T. H. (1996). Race, gender, and opportunity: A study of compensation attainment and the establishment of mentoring relationships. *Journal of Applied Psychology, 81*(3), 297–308.

Eisenhart, M. (1998). On the subject of interpretive reviews. *Review of Educational Research, 68*(4), 389–397.

Employment Discrimination Coordinator. (2005). *Analysis of Federal Law* (Vols. 1 and 3). Thomson/West: Eagan, MN.

Esquibel, A. (1992). *The career mobility of Chicano administrators in higher education: A fifty year replication study.* Boulder, CO: Western Interstate Commission for Higher Education.

Flowers, L. A. (2002). The impact of college racial composition on African American students' academic and social gains: Additional evidence. *Journal of College Student Development, 43,* 403–410.

Flowers, L. A. (2003). Investigating the representation of African American student affairs administrators: A preliminary study. *NASAP Journal, 6*(1), 37–46.

Flowers, L. A. (2004–2005). Retaining African-American students in higher education: An integrative review. *Journal of College Student Retention: Research, Theory and Practice, 6,* 23–35.

Flowers, L. A., and Pascarella, E. T. (2003). Cognitive effects of college: Differences between African American and Caucasian students. *Research in Higher Education, 44,* 21–49.

Fontaine, D. C., and Greenlee, S. P. (1993). Employment factors of African Americans. *Western Journal of Black Studies, 17*(3), 121–125.

Frank, J. (1981). The problem of the Black administrator. *AGB Reports, 23*(1), 20–24.

Fujimoto, M. J. (1996). The community college presidency: An Asian American perspective. *New Directions for Community Colleges, 94,* 47–56.

Gorena, M. (1996). *Hispanic women in higher education administration: Factors that positively influence or hinder advancement to leadership positions.* Paper presented at an annual meeting of the American Educational Research Association, April 8–12, New York, NY.

Green, P. S. (1997). Rites of passage and rights of way: A woman administrator's experiences. In L. Benjamin (Ed.) *Black women in the academy: Promises and perils* (pp. 147–157). Gainesville: University Press of Florida.

Greenhaus, J. H., and Parasuraman, S. (1993). Job performance attributions and career advancement prospects: An examination of gender and race effects. *Organizational Behavior and Human Decision Processes, 55*(2), 273–297.

Greenhaus, J. H., Parasuraman, S., and Wormley, W. M. (1990). Effects of race on organizational experiences, job performance evaluations, and career outcomes. *Academy of Management Journal, 33*(1), 64–86.

Grutter v. *Bollinger,* 539 U.S. 306 (2003).

Hamilton, K. (2002). Once-in-a-lifetime career opportunities. *Black Issues in Higher Education, 19*(20), 20–23, 26.

Haro, R. (1990). Latino and executive positions in higher education. *Educational Record, 71*(3), 39–42.

Harvard, P. (1986). *Successful behaviors of black women administrators in higher education: Implications for leadership.* Paper presented at an annual meeting of the American Educational Research Association, April 16–20, San Francisco.

Harvey, W. B. (2002). *Minorities in higher education, 2001–2002: Nineteenth annual status report.* Washington, DC: American Council on Education.

Harvey, W. B. (2005). *Minorities in higher education: Twenty-first annual status report (2003–2004).* Washington, DC: American Council on Education.

Holmes, L. S., Ebbers, L. H., Robinson, D. C., and Mugenda, A. B. (2000). Validating African-American students at predominantly white institutions. *Journal of College Student Retention, 2*(1), 41–58.

Holmes, S. L. (2004). An overview of African American college presidents: A game of two steps forward, one step backward, and standing still. *Journal of Negro Education, 73*(1), 21–39.

Howard-Hamilton, M. F., and Williams, V. A. (1996). *Assessing the environment for women of color in student affairs.* Paper prepared for Florida University, Gainsville, Office of Affirmative Action.

Howard-Vital, M. R. (1987, December). Black women in higher education: Struggling to gain visibility. *Journal of Black Studies, 20,* 180–191.

Hurtado, S., Milem, J., Clayton-Pedersen, A., and Allen, W. R. (1999). *Enacting diverse learning environments: Improving the climate for racial/ethnic diversity in higher education.* ASHE-ERIC Higher Education Report, Volume 26, No. 8. Washington, DC: The George Washington University, Graduate School of Education and Human Development, 1999.

Irvine, J. (1978). A case of double jeopardy: The Black woman in higher educational administration. *Emergent Leadership, 2*(2), 61–66.

Jackson, G. B. (1980). Methods for integrative reviews. *Review of Educational Research, 50,* 438–460.

Jackson, J.F.L. (2001). A new test for diversity: Retaining African American administrators at predominantly White institutions. In L. Jones (Ed.), *Retaining African Americans in higher education: Challenging paradigms for retaining students, faculty, and administrators* (pp. 93–109). Sterling, VA: Stylus Publishing.

Jackson, J.F.L. (2002). Retention of African American administrators at predominantly White institutions: Using professional growth factors to inform the discussion. *College and University, 78*(2), 11–16.

Jackson, J.F.L. (2003a). Engaging, retaining, and advancing African Americans in student affair administration: An analysis of employment status. *National Association of Student Affairs Professionals Journal, 6*(1), 9–23.

Jackson, J.F.L. (2003b). Toward administrative diversity: An analysis of the African-American male educational pipeline. *Journal of Men's Studies, 12*(1), 43–60.

Jackson, J.F.L. (2004a). An emerging engagement, retention, and advancement (ERA) model for African American administrators at predominantly White institutions. In D. Cleveland

(Ed.), *A long way to go: Conversations about race by African American faculty and graduate students in higher education* (pp. 211–222). New York: Peter Lang.

Jackson, J.F.L. (2004b). Engaging, retaining, and advancing African Americans in executive-level positions: A descriptive and trend analysis of academic administrators in higher and postsecondary education. *Journal of Negro Education, 73*(1), 4–20.

Jackson, J.F.L. (2004c). Top line: A status report on African American leadership in higher and postsecondary education. *Journal of Negro Education, 73*(1), 1–3.

Jackson, J.F.L. (2006a). Hiring practices of African American males in academic leadership positions at American colleges and universities: An employment trends and disparate impact analysis. *Teachers College Record, 108*(2), 316–338.

Jackson, J.F.L. (2006b). The Nature of Academic Deans' Work: Moving Toward an Academic Executive Behavioral Model in Higher Education. *Journal of the Professoriate, 1*(1), 7–22.

Jackson, J.F.L. (2008). Race segregation across the academic workforce: Exploring factors that may contribute to the disparate representation of African American men. *American Behavioral Scientist, 51,* 1004–1029.

Jackson, J.F.L., and Contreras, C. (forthcoming). Applying an engagement, retention, and advancement model for administrators of color in higher education. In C. Lewis and V. B. Bush (Eds.), *African Americans in higher education organizations: Using cultural capital to shape the future.* Sterling, VA: Stylus Publishing.

Jackson, J.F.L., and Daniels, B. D. (2006). A pilot study of the workplace experiences for white student affairs professionals at historically Black colleges and universities: Implications for organizational culture and future research. *NASAP Journal, 8*(1), 26–49.

Jackson, J.F.L., and Flowers, L. A. (2003). Retaining African American student affairs administrators: Voices from the field. *College Student Affairs Journal, 22*(2), 125–136.

Jackson, J.F.L., and O'Callaghan, F. M. (2009). What do we know about the glass ceiling effect? A taxonomy and critical review to inform higher education research. *Research in Higher Education, 50*(5), 460–482.

Jackson, J.F.L., and Rosas, M. (1999). Scholars of color: Are universities derailing their scholarship? *Keeping our Faculties Conference Proceedings* (pp. 86–107). Minneapolis: University of Minnesota.

Jenifer, F. G. (2005). *Minorities and women in higher education and the role mentoring plays in their advancement.* Austin: Office of Academic Affairs, University of Texas System.

Johnson, G. G. (1998). African American women administrators as mentors: Significance and strategies. *Initiatives, 58*(3), 49–56.

Johnson, J. R. (1997). An African American female senior-level administrator: Facing the challenges of a major research university. In L. Benjamin (Ed.) *Black women in the academy: Promises and perils* (pp. 279–290). Gainesville: University Press of Florida.

Johnsrud, L. K., and DesJarlais, C. D. (1994). Barriers to tenure for women and minorities. *Review of Higher Education, 54*(2), 123–144.

Jones, C. P. (2000). Levels of racism: A theoretical framework and a gardener's tale. *American Journal of Public Health, 90*(8), 1212–1215.

Jones, M. C. (1997). Does leadership transcend gender and race? The case of African American women college presidents. In L. Benjamin (Ed.) *Black women in the academy: Promises and perils* (pp. 201–209). Gainesville: University Press of Florida.

June, A. W. (2007). Presidents: Same look, different decade. *Chronicle of Higher Education, 53*(24), A33.

Kanter, R. M. (1977). *Men and women of the corporation.* New York: Basics Books.

Kaplin, W. A., and Lee, B. A. (1995). *The law of higher education* (3rd ed.). San Francisco: Jossey-Bass.

Kern-Foxworth, M. (2000). Beyond gender: The experience of women of color. In D. M. Smith (Ed.), *Women at work: Leadership for the next century* (pp. 80–100). Upper Saddle River, NJ: Prentice Hall.

Kidder, W. C., and Rossner, J. (2002). How the SAT creates "built-in-headwinds": An educational and legal analysis of disparate impact. *Santa Clara Law Review, 43,* 131–211.

King, D. (1988). Multiple jeopardy, multiple consciousness: The context of a black feminist ideology. *Signs 14*(1), 42–72.

Konrad, A. M., and Pfeffer, J. (1991, July). Understanding the hiring of women and minorities in educational institutions. *Sociology of Education, 64,* 141–157.

Kraiger, K., and Ford, J. K. (1985). A meta-analysis of ratee race effects in performing ratings. *Journal of Applied Psychology, 70,* 56–65.

Lee, J. (1997). Characteristics of college and university staff. *National Education Association Update, 3*(4).Washington, DC: National Education Association.

Leon, D. (Ed.). (2005). *Lessons in leadership: Executive leadership programs for advancing diversity in higher education.* New York: Elsevier/JAI Press.

Lindsay, B. (1994). African American women and *Brown*: A lingering twilight or emerging dawn? *Journal of Negro Education, 63*(3), 430–442.

Lindsay, B. (1997). Surviving the middle passage: The absent legacy of African American women education deans? In L. A. Castenell and J. M. Tarule (Eds.) *The minority voice in educational reform: An analysis by minority and women college of education deans* (pp. 3–31). Greenwich, CT: Ablex Publishing.

Lindsay, B. (1999). Women chief executives and their approaches towards equity in American universities. *Comparative Education, 35*(2), 187–199.

Livers, A. B., and Caver, K. A. (2003). *Leading in Black and White: Working across the racial divide in corporate America.* San Francisco: Jossey-Bass.

Lynch, P. D., and Charleston, M. (1990). The emergence of American Indian leadership in education. *Journal of American Indian Education, 29*(2), 1–10.

Martinez, R. O. (1999). *Hispanic leadership in American higher education.* Paper commissioned by the Hispanic Association of Colleges and Universities. San Antonio: Hispanic Association of Colleges and Universities.

Martinez, R. O. (2005). Latino demographic and institutional issues in higher education: Implications for leadership development. In D. Leon (Ed.), *Lessons in leadership: Executive leadership programs for advancing diversity in higher education* (pp. 85–105). New York: Elsevier/JAI Press.

Mason, M. A., and Goulden, M. (2002). Do babies matter? *Academe, 88*(6), 21–28.

Mason, M. A., and Goulden, M. (2004a). Do babies matter? (Part II): Closing the baby gap. *Academe, 90*(6), 11–16.

Mason, M. A., and Goulden, M. (2004b). Marriage and baby blues: Redefining gender equity in the academy. *Annals of the American Association of Political and Social Scientists, 596,* 86–103.

Maume, D. J., Jr. (2004). Is the glass ceiling a unique form of inequality? Evidence from a random-effects model of managerial attainment. *Work and Occupations, 31*(2), 250–274.

McCabe, B. C., and Stream, C. (2000). Diversity by the numbers. *Public Personnel Management, 29*(1), 93–107.

McCall, L. (2005). The complexity of intersectionality. *Signs: Journal of Women and Culture in Society, 30*(3), 1771–1800.

McCurtis, B. R., Jackson, J.F.L., and O'Callaghan, E. M. (2009). Developing leaders of color in higher education: Can contemporary programs address historical employment trends? In A. Kezar (Ed.), *Rethinking leadership in a complex, multicultural and global environment* (pp. 65–92). Sterling, VA: Stylus Publishing.

McRae, M. B., and Carter, R. T. (1992). Occupational profiles of Blacks in management: Implications for career counseling. *Journal of Employment Counseling, 29,* 2–4.

Meier, K. J. (1975). Representative bureaucracy: An empirical analysis. *American Political Science Review, 69*(2), 526–542.

Meier, K. J. (1993a). Latinos and representative bureaucracy: Testing the Thompson and Henderson hypotheses. *Journal of Public Administration Research and Theory, 3,* 393–414.

Meier, K. J. (1993b). Representative bureaucracy: A theoretical and empirical exposition. In J. Perry (Ed.), *Research in Public Administration.* Greenwich CT: JAI Press.

Meier, K. J., and Bohte, J. (2001). Structure and the performance of public organizations: Task difficulty and span of control. *Public Organization Review 1,* 341–354.

Meier, K. J., and Nigro, L. G. (1976). Representative bureaucracy and policy preferences: A study in the attitudes of federal executives. *Public Administration Review, 36,* 458–469.

Meier, K. J., and Stewart, J., Jr. (1992). Active representation in educational bureaucracies: Policy impacts. *American Review of Public Administration, 22,* 157–71.

Merisotis, J. P., and Aveilhe, K. (2005). The Kellog MSI leadership fellows program. In D. J. Leon (Ed.), *Lessons in leadership: Executive leadership programs for advancing diversity in higher education* (pp. 207–222). New York: Elsevier/JAI Press.

Miller, K. T. (1991). Formula for success: A study of minorities in academe who are making it. *CUPA Journal, 42,* 27–33.

Minor, J. T. (2008). Segregation residual in higher education: A tale of two states. *American Educational Research Journal, 45*(4), 861–885.

Mitchell, P. T. (Ed.). (1993). *Cracking the wall: Women in higher education administration.* Washington, DC: College and University Personnel Association.

Montez, J. M. (1998). *Asian/Pacific American women in higher education administration: Doubly bound, doubly scarce.* Issues in Policy (No. 9). Pullman: Washington State University.

Moore, L. (2005). Should I apply? A college marketing director mulls whether to take the next step and seek a vice presidency. *Chronicle of Higher Education, 52*(15), C2.

Moore, W., Jr., and Wagstaff, L. H. (1974). *Black educators in white colleges.* San Francisco: Jossey-Bass.

Mosley, M. H. (1980). Black women administrators in higher education: An endangered species. *Journal of Black Studies, 10*(3), 295–310.

Mulnix, M. W., Bowden, R. G., and Lopez, E. E. (2002). A brief examination of institutional advancement activities at Hispanic serving institutions. *Journal of Hispanic Higher Education, 1*(2), 174–190.

Myers, E. M., and Sandeen, A. (1973). Survey of minority and women student affairs staff members employed in NASPA member institutions. *NASPA Journal, 11*(1), 2–14.

Nakanishi, D. T. (1993). Asian Pacific Americans in higher education: Faculty and administrative representation and tenure. *New Directions for Teaching and Learning, 53,* 51–59.

Nettles, M. T., and Perna, L. W. (1997). *The African American educational data book* (Volume 1). Fairfax, VA: Frederick D. Patterson Institute.

O'Callaghan, E. M. (2007). Unintended consequences: Examining sex-based discrimination and the tenure process. *Journal of the Professoriate, 2*(1), 53–74.

Pascarella, E. T., and Terenzini, P. T. (2005). *How college affects students: A third decade of research.* San Francisco: Jossey-Bass.

Perez, M. G. (2004). Fair and facially neutral higher educational admissions through disparate impact analysis. *Michigan Journal of Race and Law, 9,* 467–502.

Pierce, D. R., Mahoney, J. R., and Kee, A. M. (1996). Professional development resources for minority administrators. *New Directions for Community Colleges, 94,* 81–92.

Powell, J. V. (1991). Increasing equity in administrative leadership: A regent's model. *Equity and Excellence, 25*(2–4), 67–76.

Reis, P., and Thurgood, D. H. (1993). *Summary report 1991: Doctorate recipients from United States universities.* Washington, DC: National Academy Press.

Rolle, K. A., Davies, T. G., and Banning, J. H. (2000). African American administrators' experiences in predominantly White colleges and universities. *Journal of Research and Practice, 24,* 79–94.

Rusher, A. (1996). *African American women administrators.* Lanham, MD: University Press of America.

Sanders, K. W., and Mellow, G. O. (1990). Permanent diversity: The deferred vision of higher education. *Initiatives, 53*(1), 9–13.

Sandler, B. R. (1986). *The campus climate revisited: Chilly for women faculty, administrators, and graduate students.* Washington, DC: Association of American Colleges.

Selmi, M. (2006). Was the disparate impact theory a mistake? *University of California–Los Angeles Law Review, 53,* 701–782.

Simpson, B. (2000). *Can't you lighten up a bit? Black women administrators in the academy.* Paper presented at the Annual National Conference of the National Association of

African American Studies and the National Association of Hispanic and Latino Studies, February 21–26, Houston, TX.

Singh, K., Robinson, A., and Williams-Greene, J. (1995). Differences in perceptions of African American women and men faculty and administrators. *Journal of Negro Education, 64*(4), 401–408.

Smith, C. H. (1980). The peculiar status of Black educational administrators: The university setting. *Journal of Black Studies, 10*(3), 323–334.

Suggs, W. (2005). Faces in a mostly white, male crowd. *Chronicle of Higher Education, 51*(31), A34.

Swisher, K. G. (2001). Solid ground: Comment on "Shifting sands: Reflections from the field of higher education." *Anthropology and Education Quarterly, 32*(4), 502–506.

Tannen, D. (1994). *Gender and discourse.* New York: Oxford University Press.

Tannen, D. (Ed.). (1998). *Linguistics in context: Connecting observation and understanding.* New York: Ablex Publishing.

Thelin, J. R. (2004). *A history of American higher education.* Baltimore: Johns Hopkins University Press.

Thomas, D. A., and Gabarro, J. J. (1999). *Breaking through: The making of minority executives in corporate America.* Boston: Harvard Business School Press.

Thomas, J. (2005). African American leadership in higher education. In D. J. Leon (Ed.), *Lessons in leadership: Executive leadership programs for advancing diversity in higher education* (pp. 85–105). New York: Elsevier/JAI Press.

Thompson, T. E., and Bjork, L. G. (1989). *A collaborative approach to preparing minority administrators.* Paper presented at an annual meeting of the Southern Regional Council on Educational Administration, November 11–14, Columbia, SC.

Thornton, S. (2005). Making graduate school more parent friendly. *Academe, 91*(6), 69–70.

Trix, F., and Psenka, C. (2003). Exploring the color of glass. Letters of recommendation for female and male medical faculty. *Discourse & Society, 14,* 191–220.

Tucker, C. H. (1980). The cycle, dilemma and expectations of the black administrator. *Journal of Black Studies, 10*(3), 311–321.

Turner, C.S.V., and Myers, S. L. (2000). *Faculty of color in academe: Bittersweet success.* Needham Heights, MA: Allyn & Bacon.

Twombly, S. B. (1998). Women academic leaders in a Latin American university: Reconciling the paradoxes of professional lives. *Higher Education, 35,* 367–397.

U.S. Census Bureau. (June, 2001). Mapping Census 2000: The Geography of U.S. Diversity. Retrieved September 2009, from http://www.census.gov/population/www/cen2000/atlas/pdf/censr01-104.pdf.

U.S. Commission on Civil Rights. (1995). *Briefing paper for the U.S. Commission on Civil Rights: Legislative, executive and judicial development of affirmative action* (NCJ No. 156021). Washington, DC: Office of the General Counsel.

U. S. Department of Education. (2002). *The gender and racial/ethnic composition of postsecondary instructional faculty and staff, 1992–1998.* Washington, DC: National Center for Education Statistics.

University of California v. *Bakke,* 438 U.S. 265 (1978).

Ward, K. A., and Wolf-Wendel, L. (2004). Academic motherhood: Managing complex roles in research universities. *Review of Higher Education, 27*(2), 233–257.

Warner, L. S. (1995). A study of American Indian females in higher education administration. *Initiatives, 56*(4), 11–17.

Watson, L. W. (2001). In their voices: A glimpse of African-American women administrators in higher education. *NASPA Journal, 4*(1), 7–16.

Weinberg, S. L. (2008). Monitoring faculty diversity: The need for a more granular approach. *Journal of Higher Education, 79*(4), 365–387.

Williams, A. (1986). *A profile of Black female administrators at a large urban public university.* Paper presented at an annual meeting of the American Educational Research Association, April 16–20, San Francisco, CA.

Williams, A. (1989). Research on Black women college administrators: Descriptive and interview data. *Sex Roles, 21*(1/2), 99–112.

Wilson, R. (1989). Women of color in academic administration: Trends, progress, and barriers. *Sex Roles, 21*(1/2), 85–97.

Wilson, S. J. (1977). Survey of minority and women student affairs staff members employed in NASPA member institutions in 1974. *NASPA Journal, 14*(10), 58–73.

Wolfman, B. R. (1997). "Light as from a beacon": African American women administrators in the academy. In L. Benjamin (Ed.), *Black women in the academy: Promises and perils* (pp. 158–167). Gainesville: University Press of Florida.

Name Index

Nigro, L. G., 35
Nkomo, S. M., 37, 40, 44, 51, 52

O

O'Callaghan, E. M., 9, 12, 34, 36, 37, 43, 45, 52, 53, 54, 57, 71
Ovadia, S., 36

P

Parasuraman, S., 45
Pascarella, E. T., 8, 9
Perez, M. G., 34
Perna, L. W., 8
Pfeffer, J., 2, 7, 11, 67
Pierce, D. R., 54
Powell, J. V., 7, 53

R

Reis, P., 48
Richey, D., 8, 31, 39, 42, 57, 60
Robinson, A., 1, 43, 45
Rolle, K. A., 41, 60, 61, 68
Rosas, M., 1
Rossner, J., 34
Rusher, A., 47

S

Sandeen, A., 2
Sanders, K. W., 58
Sandler, B. R., 45
Selmi, M., 34
Simpson, B., 49
Singh, K., 43, 45, 68
Smith, C. H., 66, 67
Stewart, J., Jr., 4, 35
Stockdale, M. S., 55

Suggs, W., 2
Swisher, K. G., 53

T

Tannen, D., 45
Terenzini, P. T., 8
Thelin, J. R., 8
Thomas, D. A., 49, 50, 52, 53, 54
Thompson, T. E., 53
Thornton, S., 43
Thurgood, D. H., 48
Tucker, C. H., 50, 51, 67
Twombly, S. B., 42, 59

U

University of California v. Bakke, 32

V

Vanneman, R., 36

W

Wagstaff, L. H., 44
Walker, H., 48
Ward, K. A., 44, 59
Warner, L. S., 29, 43, 53
Watson, L. W., 37, 38, 39, 40, 44, 72
Weinberg, S. L., 32, 34, 35
Williams, A., 42, 57
Williams, V. A., 31, 39, 60, 68
Williams–Greene, J., 43, 45, 68
Wilson, R., 7, 43, 44, 68
Wilson, S. J., 2
Wolfman, B. R., 37, 42, 43, 61
Wolf–Wendel, L., 59
Wormley, W. M., 45

Subject Index

A

Academic leaders: average age of, 13; distribution by age, race/ethnicity, 14; distribution by gender/credentials/race/ethnicity, 13; publications/presentations in career by race/ethnicity, 22; selection process for, 20–21

Activities by race/ethnicity, 14–15, 29

Administrators of color, 29–30; African American, 37, 51; aggregated challenges for, 68–71; backgrounds of, 50; barriers encountered by, 7–8; Black women as, 43–45; characteristics for, 61–62; emergent challenges for, 66–68; emerging model for, 62–64; emotional aspects for female, 51–52; engagement/retention/advancement overview, 8–9; ethnic composition of, 4; female, 48; legal and conceptual frameworks for underrepresentation of, 32–36; mentoring for, 54–57; preparation for rejection by, 61; by region, 30; social barriers to advancement, 38–41; strategies for individuals, 60–62; underrepresentation of, 12; understanding causes of, 38

Advancement process, 48, 50, 72; engagement, retention, and advancement model, 62–64; factors influencing, 49; leadership programs/professional associations, 52–53; strategies for universities, 57–60

Affirmative action, 32–34, 33, 57–58, 67, 71–72, 73

Age cohort gaps, 30

Age distribution of academic leaders, 13, 14

Aggregated challenges for administrators of color, 68–71

Alliance for Equity in Higher Education, 54

American Council on Education, 7

American Indian Higher Education Consortium, 54

B

Balance between work and life, 59, 71–72

Barriers for administrators of color: concentric influence of, 39; established, 37–43; female African American, 51; frameworks for discussing, 32–36; identification of, 72–73; multiple categories of, 45–46; overview, 7–8, 31–32; persistent, 73–74; relationship between organization and individual, 42; women of color and, 43–45

Black institutions, 44

Breaking Through (Thomas and Gabarro), 50

C

Campus environment, 56–57, 58, 71–72

Career advancement: of administrators of color, 8–9; barriers to, 7–8, 44; measurability of, 63–64; mentoring, 56; race and gender differences in, 45, 68;

strategies for, 60–62; university support for, 57–60

Caring fields, 17

Carnegie classification by race/ethnicity, 19

Challenges: aggregated, 68–71; emergent, 66–68; employment/engagement/recruitment, 47–49; persistent, 73–74; reviewing, 73

Civil Rights Act of 1991, 36

Company identity, 50

Conceptual frameworks for underrepresentation of administrators of color, 32–36

Corporate America, 49–52

D

Degree attainment: distribution of student affairs administrators by, 22–23; by gender/race, 13; by race/ethnicity, 18–19

Demographic composition of students, 35

Department of Labor, 36

Development process, 50

Discrimination: double discrimination dilemma, 44, 47, 56, 61; factors contributing to, 39; identification criteria for, 36; lawsuits, 34; by race or gender, 40–41, 44–45

Disparate impact theory, 33, 34

Diversity: call for change, 74; of campus environment, 57–58; importance of, 3–5, 9; levels of, 35; status of, 7

Double discrimination dilemma, 44, 47, 56, 61

E

Emergent challenges for administrators of color, 66–68

Emotional issues of African American women, 51–52

Employment: challenges of, 47–49; section rankings, 68–71; status by race/ethnicity, 17–18

Employment Discrimination Coordinator, 34

Engagement, retention, and advancement model, 62–64, 72

Engagement of administrators of color, 8–9, 47–49

Engagement phase of administrator model, 62–63

Ethnicity: academic leaders distribution by, 14; degree attainment by, 13; income data by, 71; mode and mean data by for student affairs administrators, 70; student affairs administrators distribution by, 23, 24, 25, 27, 28; workforce mode and mean data by, 69

Executives of color. See administrators of color

Extended family ethnic, 43

F

Faculty of color, retention of, 4–5

Family issues, 42–43, 59

Females. See gender

Flexibility in leadership positions, 59

Formal mentoring, 55

Full-time academic leaders by race/ethnicity, 16, 18, 19, 20

Full-time student affairs administrators: distribution by institutional size, income, race/ethnicity, 24, 25, 27; distribution by position, race/ethnicity, 28; highest credentials attained by, 23

Future research directions, 37, 71–72

G

Gender: African American males, 41; African American women in higher education, 39–40; barriers for minority women, 39–40, 43–45, 44–45; communication differences, 45; discrimination based on, 44–45; distribution of academic leaders by, 13; distribution of student affairs administrators by, 22–23; flexibility for women, 59; glass ceiling concept, 35–36; internal barriers by, 42–43; mode and mean data by for student affairs administrators, 70; numbers of African American females versus males in higher education, 48; reverse gap in administrative positions, 30; segregation by, 66; workforce mode and mean data by, 69

Glass ceiling concept, 33, 35–36, 50

H

Hiring process, 60, 71–72, 73

Hispanic Association of Colleges and Universities, 54

I

Implications for practice, 72–73

Income: of academic leaders by race/ethnicity, 16, 17; difference based on gender, 44; mean income data by race, 70; sex–based differences in, 44–45; of student affairs administrators by race/ethnicity, 23, 24

Individual barriers for administrators of color, 42

Informal mentoring, 55

Institutional control: distribution of academic leaders by, 20; student affairs administrators distribution by, 25

Institutional/organizational barriers to success, 38, 41–42

Institutional programs and initiatives, 71–72

Institutional size, distribution of student affairs administrators by, 24

Institutional type (public/private): student affairs administrators distribution by, 25; workforce distribution by, 19–20

Internal barriers for administrators of color, 42–43, 45–46

K

Kellogg Minority Serving Institutions Leadership Fellows Program, 54

Kennedy, John F., 32

L

Leadership opportunities: qualifications for, 60–61; support by institutions for, 71–72

Leadership programs, role of, 52–54

Legal frameworks, 32–36

Levels of racial and ethnic diversity, 35

Linguistics research, 45

Literature review, 5–6; administrative leadership programs, 53; barriers to success, 45–46; business and organizational management, 52

M

Males. *See* gender

Mentoring, 54–57, 67, 71–72

Minority group representation in United States, 29

Multicultural campus environments, 57–58

N

National Association for Equal Opportunity in Higher Education, 54

National Association of Student Personnel Administrators (NASPA): regions analyzed, 26; Salary Survey, 11, 12, 23, 24, 25, 27, 28, 70

National data analysis, 29–30

National Study of Postsecondary Faculty (NSOPF:99), 11, 12

Nesting concept, 38

O

Organizational/institutional barriers for administrators of color, 41–42

Orientation phase of administrator model, 62

Our Separate Ways (Bell and Nkomo), 51

Outcomes phase of administrator model, 63–64

P

Part–time academic leaders by race/ethnicity, 16, 20

Peer mentoring, 55–56

Performance indicators, 20, 22

Pipeline problem, 48

Position type: affirmative action and, 67; for African American women, 48; barriers to upper level, 37; distribution by NASPA region, 26; factors influencing appointments, 49; gender differences in, 44–45; satisfaction with, by race and gender, 40; student affairs administrators distribution by, 28; underrepresentation of people of color by, 41–42

Practice implications, 72–73

Preengagement phase of administrator model, 62

Private institutions: percentage of workforce in, 19–20; student affairs administrators distribution by, 25

Professional associations, 52–53, 73

Professional development, 67–68

Program areas by race/ethnicity, 16–17

Promotion process, fairness in, 60

Protected classes, 34

Public institutions: percentage of workforce in, 19–20; student affairs administrators distribution by, 25

Published works, 48–49

R

Race: centrality of, 41, 50–51; consideration for hiring/admissions decisions by, 33; degree attainment by, 13; distribution of academic leaders by, 14; distribution of student affairs administrators by, 22–23, 24; income data by, 71; mode and mean data by for student affairs administrators, 70; by NASPA region, 26; segregation by, 66; student affairs administrators distribution by, 25, 27, 28; theoretical perspectives on, 32; work activities by, 29; workforce mode and mean data by, 69

Race–based glass ceiling, 50

Racial diversity as company identity, 50

Racial identity, 50–51

Racism, 40, 43–45, 48–49, 66–67

Rank of academic leaders by race/ethnicity, 15–16, 68, 71

Recruitment efforts by institutions, 14; challenges of, 47–49; fairness in, 60; strategies for universities, 57–60

Region: administrators of color by, 30;

full–time academic leaders by, 21; NASPA's delineation of, 26; student affairs administrators distribution by, 27

Representative bureaucracy theory, 4, 33, 35

Research participation by race/ethnicity, 15

Retention, 72; of administrators of color, 8–9, 56–57; engagement, retention, and advancement model, 62–64; fairness in, 60; of female faculty, 59; measure of, 63–64; planning for, 4; strategies for universities, 57–60; for students/faculty of color, 4–5

Retirement age, 30

Rites of Passage and Rights of Way (Green), 54

S

Segregation, 66

Selection process for academic leaders, 20, 22

Sexism, 45

Size of institution, student affairs administrators distribution by, 23, 24, 28

Social barriers to advancement, 38–41

Status of women of color, 51

Strategies for individual administrators, 60–62

Student affairs administrators: distribution by race/ethnicity and size of institution, 28; distribution by size of institution, 23; gender distribution, 22–23; income by race/ethnicity, 24; income data on, 71; mode and mean data by race or ethnicity for, 70; retention of, 56–57

Students: demographic composition of, 35; retention of, 4–5

Support by institutions/organizations, 71–72

Support groups, 57, 61, 67

Survey of Doctorate Recipients, 59

T

Tenure, 45, 48, 59

Terminology/search terms, 5–6

Three–tiered approach to institutional diversity, 5, 35

Token syndrome, 41, 48
Training programs for leadership, 53–54
Trend analysis, distribution of full–time
administrative positions, 12

U

Underutilization analysis, 33, 34
United States: minority group
representation in, 29; segregation in, 66;
Supreme Court decisions, 32
U.S. Commission on Civil Rights, 32
U.S. Department of Education, 12, 13, 14,
15, 16, 17, 18, 19, 20, 21, 22, 48

University of California Faculty Work and
Family Survey, 59
University support for career advancement,
57–60

W

White institutions, 7–8, 44, 57–58, 72
W. K. Kellogg Foundation, 54
Women. *See* gender
Work activities by race/ethnicity, 14–15
Workforce, mode and mean data by race or
ethnicity, 69
Workforce 2000 (Department of Labor), 36

About the Authors

Jerlando F. L. Jackson is associate professor of higher and postsecondary education in educational leadership and policy analysis at the University of Wisconsin–Madison. He also serves as coordinator for the Higher, Post-secondary, and Continuing Education Program. Jackson's central research interests are workforce diversity and workplace discrimination in higher education. Frequently sought as a keynote speaker, he is credited with more than 90 publications, 125 presentations, and several edited volumes.

Elizabeth M. O'Callaghan is a doctoral student and research associate at the University of Wisconsin in the Educational Leadership and Policy Analysis Department. She has published articles and book chapters in the areas of gender equity in the tenure process, the experiences of women and girls in science and engineering disciplines, and campus-based violence against women. Previously, O'Callaghan worked at a women's foundation in Washington, DC, and as assistant to the associate dean at Teachers College, Columbia University.

About the ASHE Higher Education Report Series

Since 1983, the ASHE (formerly ASHE-ERIC) Higher Education Report Series has been providing researchers, scholars, and practitioners with timely and substantive information on the critical issues facing higher education. Each monograph presents a definitive analysis of a higher education problem or issue, based on a thorough synthesis of significant literature and institutional experiences. Topics range from planning to diversity and multiculturalism, to performance indicators, to curricular innovations. The mission of the Series is to link the best of higher education research and practice to inform decision making and policy. The reports connect conventional wisdom with research and are designed to help busy individuals keep up with the higher education literature. Authors are scholars and practitioners in the academic community. Each report includes an executive summary, review of the pertinent literature, descriptions of effective educational practices, and a summary of key issues to keep in mind to improve educational policies and practice.

The Series is one of the most peer reviewed in higher education. A National Advisory Board made up of ASHE members reviews proposals. A National Review Board of ASHE scholars and practitioners reviews completed manuscripts. Six monographs are published each year and they are approximately 120 pages in length. The reports are widely disseminated through Jossey-Bass and John Wiley & Sons, and they are available online to subscribing institutions through Wiley InterScience (http://www.interscience.wiley.com).

Call for Proposals

The ASHE Higher Education Report Series is actively looking for proposals. We encourage you to contact one of the editors, Dr. Kelly Ward (kaward@wsu.edu) or Dr. Lisa Wolf-Wendel (lwolf@ku.edu), with your ideas.

Recent Titles

Volume 35 ASHE Higher Education Report

1. Bridging the Diversity Divide: Globalization and Reciprocal Empowerment in Higher Education
   Edna Chun and Alvin Evans

2. Understanding Interdisciplinary Challenges and Opportunities in Higher Education
   Karri A. Holley

Volume 34 ASHE Higher Education Report

1. Theoretical Perspectives on Student Success: Understanding the Contributions of the Disciplines
   Laura W. Perna and Scott L. Thomas

2. Selling Higher Education: Marketing and Advertising America's Colleges and Universities
   Eric J. Anctil

3. Faculty Careers and Work Lives: A Professional Growth Perspective
   KerryAnn O'Meara, Aimee LaPointe Terosky, and Anna Neumann

4. Intellectual Property in the Information Age: Knowledge as Commodity and Its Legal
   Implications for Higher Education
   Jeffrey C. Sun and Benjamin Baez

5. The Entrepreneurial Domains of Higher Education
   Matthew M. Mars and Amy Scott Metcalfe

6. The Development of Doctoral Students: Phases of Challenge and Support
   Susan K. Gardner

Volume 33 ASHE Higher Education Report

1. Are the Walls Really Down? Behavioral and Organizational Barriers to Faculty and Staff Diversity
   Alvin Evans and Edna Breinig Chun

2. Christian Faith and Scholarship: An Exploration of Contemporary Developments
   Todd C. Ream and Perry L. Glanzer

3. Economically and Educationally Challenged Students in Higher Education: Access to Outcomes
   MaryBeth Walpole

4. Reinventing Undergraduate Education: Engaging College Students in Research and Creative
   Activities
   Shouping Hu, Kathyrine Scheuch, Robert Schwartz, Joy Gaston Gayles, and Shaoqing Li

5. Academic Integrity in the Twenty-First Century: A Teaching and Learning Imperative
   Tricia Bertram Gallant

6. Parental Involvement in Higher Education: Understanding the Relationship Among Students,
   Parents, and the Institution
   Katherine Lynk Wartman and Marjorie Savage

Volume 32 ASHE Higher Education Report

1. Cost-Efficiencies in Online Learning
   Katrina A. Meyer

2. Lifelong Learning and the Academy: The Changing Nature of Continuing Education
   Jeffrey A. Cantor

3. Diversity Leadership in Higher Education
   Adalberto Aguirre, Jr., Rubén O. Martinez

4. Intergroup Dialogue in Higher Education: Meaningful Learning About Social Justice
   Ximena Zúñiga, Biren (Ratnesh) A. Nagda, Mark Chesler, and Adena Cytron-Walker

5. Piecing Together the Student Success Puzzle: Research, Propositions, and Recommendations
   George D. Kuh, Jillian Kinzie, Jennifer A. Buckley, Brian K. Bridges, and John C. Hayek

ORDER FORM SUBSCRIPTION AND SINGLE ISSUES

DISCOUNTED BACK ISSUES:

Use this form to receive 20% off all back issues of *ASHE Higher Education Report.*
All single issues priced at **$23.20** (normally $29.00)

TITLE   ISSUE NO.   ISBN

_____   _____   _____

_____   _____   _____

_____   _____   _____

*Call 888-378-2537 or see mailing instructions below. When calling, mention the promotional code JBXND
to receive your discount. For a complete list of issues, please visit www.josseybass.com/go/aehe*

SUBSCRIPTIONS: (1 YEAR, 6 ISSUES)

☐ New Order   ☐ Renewal

U.S.	☐ Individual: $174	☐ Institutional: $244
CANADA/MEXICO	☐ Individual: $174	☐ Institutional: $304
ALL OTHERS	☐ Individual: $210	☐ Institutional: $355

*Call 888-378-2537 or see mailing and pricing instructions below.
Online subscriptions are available at www.interscience.wiley.com*

ORDER TOTALS:

Issue / Subscription Amount: $ _____

Shipping Amount: $ _____
(for single issues only – subscription prices include shipping)

Total Amount: $ _____

SHIPPING CHARGES:		
SURFACE	DOMESTIC	CANADIAN
First Item	$5.00	$6.00
Each Add'l Item	$3.00	$1.50

*(No sales tax for U.S. subscriptions. Canadian residents, add GST for subscription orders. Individual rate subscriptions must
be paid by personal check or credit card. Individual rate subscriptions may not be resold as library copies.)*

BILLING & SHIPPING INFORMATION:

☐ **PAYMENT ENCLOSED:** *(U.S. check or money order only. All payments must be in U.S. dollars.)*

☐ **CREDIT CARD:**   ☐VISA   ☐MC   ☐AMEX

    Card number _____ Exp. Date_____

    Card Holder Name_____ Card Issue # *(required)* _____

    Signature _____ Day Phone_____

☐ **BILL ME:** *(U.S. institutional orders only. Purchase order required.)*

    Purchase order # _____
                  Federal Tax ID 13559302 • GST 89102-8052

Name_____

Address_____

Phone_____ E-mail_____

Copy or detach page and send to: **John Wiley & Sons, PTSC, 5th Floor
                                  989 Market Street, San Francisco, CA 94103-1741**

Order Form can also be faxed to: **888-481-2665**

PROMO JBXND

ASHE-ERIC HIGHER EDUCATION REPORT IS NOW AVAILABLE ONLINE AT WILEY INTERSCIENCE

What is Wiley InterScience?

Wiley InterScience is the dynamic online content service from John Wiley & Sons delivering the full text of over 300 leading scientific, technical, medical, and professional journals, plus major reference works, the acclaimed Current Protocols laboratory manuals, and even the full text of select Wiley print books online.

What are some special features of Wiley InterScience?

Wiley Interscience Alerts is a service that delivers table of contents via e-mail for any journal available on Wiley InterScience as soon as a new issue is published online.
Early View is Wiley's exclusive service presenting individual articles online as soon as they are ready, even before the release of the compiled print issue. These articles are complete, peer-reviewed, and citable.
CrossRef is the innovative multi-publisher reference linking system enabling readers to move seamlessly from a reference in a journal article to the cited publication, typically located on a different server and published by a different publisher.

How can I access Wiley InterScience?

Visit http://www.interscience.wiley.com.

Guest Users can browse Wiley InterScience for unrestricted access to journal Tables of Contents and Article Abstracts, or use the powerful search engine.
Registered Users are provided with a *Personal Home Page* to store and manage customized alerts, searches, and links to favorite journals and articles. Additionally, Registered Users can view free Online Sample Issues and preview selected material from major reference works.
Licensed Customers are entitled to access full-text journal articles in PDF, with select journals also offering full-text HTML.

How do I become an Authorized User?

Authorized Users are individuals authorized by a paying Customer to have access to the journals in Wiley InterScience. For example, a University that subscribes to Wiley journals is considered to be the Customer.

Faculty, staff and students authorized by the University to have access to those journals in Wiley InterScience are Authorized Users. Users should contact their Library for information on which Wiley journals they have access to in Wiley InterScience.

ASK YOUR INSTITUTION ABOUT WILEY INTERSCIENCE TODAY!

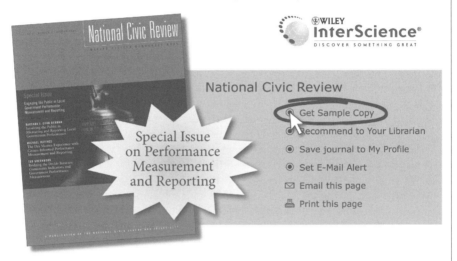